THE
GREATEST
THING IN THE
WORLD
LOVE

THE
GREATEST
THING IN THE
WORLD
LOVE

HENRY DRUMMOND

REWRITTEN AND EXPANDED BY
HAROLD J. CHADWICK

Bridge-Logos *Publishers*

Gainesville, Florida 32614 USA

The Greatest Thing in the World . . . Love.
By Henry Drummond with Harold J. Chadwick
Copyright© 1999 by Bridge-Logos Publishers
Reprinted 2001
Library of Congress Catalog Card Number:
International Standard Book Number: 0-88270-763-9

Published by:

Bridge-Logos *Publishers*

P.O. Box 141630
Gainesville, FL 32614, USA
www.bridgelogos.com

TABLE OF CONTENTS

PREFACE

Why publish a Pure Gold Classic version of a book that has already lasted for over 115 years? Several reasons.

The first and foremost reason is that Henry Drummond's book, *The Greatest Thing in the World*, deserves to be a Pure Gold Classic book. The book has been copied and recopied a thousand times since Dwight Moody published it in 1884, with virtually no publisher investing the time and money to give it the creative treatment it should have and rightly deserves. As a result, almost without exception, Drummond's classic on the most important element of Christianity has deteriorated into cheaply and badly produced pocket editions that are published simply for the sake of publishing them. It should not be so.

In the secular world, most classics are available as quality books that any reader would be proud to keep on his or her bookshelf. Not so in Christianity. We publish our classics as throwaway books. It is our intention at Bridge-Logos Publishers, however, to change that, and to publish a series of Pure Gold Classics books that Christian readers will proudly keep on their bookshelves and read time and again, both for the inspiration and knowledge they obtain, and because they are enjoyable to have and to read.

Another reason is that Drummond's material was hand copied at a meeting where he taught on love—the material was not written for a book. As a result, the material, as with any spoken material, tends to wander and is sometimes difficult to follow. In this Pure Gold Classic, the material has been revised and formatted so that it reads as it would if Drummond had written it specifically for a book. In so doing, nothing has been lost, and his material is now easier to follow and read.

The third reason is that since 1884, when *The Greatest Thing in the World* was originally published, some of its words have become archaic, and so they were replaced with their modern equivalent. Also, many of the people, places, and other items, such as the *Pickwick Papers*, are no longer well-known or known at all. We've included information about most of these historical references in the endnotes.

A fourth reason is that while he was doing his teaching, Drummond apparently quoted Scripture verses from memory. In so doing, he seems to have quoted from a combination of the original Revised Standard Version and the King James Version—and sometimes from one or the other or both plus his own version. To correct this problem, the Scripture version that most closely followed a particular text was used to replace his mixed quotation. In each case, the version that is used is noted in the Endnotes. When no version is noted the scripture is taken from the New King James Version.

Reason five is that none of the editions of Drummond's book that I read contained Scripture references for the Scriptures that he quoted, so if a reader wishes to check the quotation in the Bible, he or she has do a word search each time—unless, of course, they know the Scripture. Without a computer, a continual word search can get a bit tedious and frustrating. So in the Endnotes we have included the Scripture references for every Scripture quotation.

The sixth reason is that in 1 Corinthians 13, Paul used a Greek word for love that Jesus had defined and elevated to mean *God's kind of love*—the Greek word is *agape*. But Paul did not explain in his epistle what this type of love was, probably because it was well understood in the Church at that time, having been spoken of often by Jesus and undoubtedly taught verbally by Paul. Drummond did not explain it either. So it is assumed, likely by most, that the type of love referred to in 1 Corinthians 13 is the love that is meant when someone says to someone else, "I love you." But that is seldom so. For that reason, we have added four chapters to Drummond's book that deal exclusively with this special type of love—*agape.*

In addition, since other Scriptures help us to best understand the meaning of a Scripture, or the meaning of words in the Bible, we have also included an Addendum that contains 579 Scripture verses from Nave's Topical Bible that refer directly to love or are related to love, according to Nave. Many of them do not talk about love, but show love in action, such as the Scriptures from Genesis about Abram and Lot. To help you to explore and understand *agape*, we have boldfaced many, but not all, of the verses and passages that specifically show or speak of this type of love.

Lastly, we have included a comprehensive Index to help you find the various topics, places, and people in the book.

It is our hope that by doing all this, you will find this Pure Gold Classic version of Drummond's book, now titled *The Greatest Thing in the World...Love,* to be much more than just another copy of his book. We hope you will find it to be a manual on God's kind of love that will lead you deep into understanding it and manifesting it in your life. If that is so, then all the effort we have put into this book will be well worthwhile.

Harold J. Chadwick

SECTION 1

THE GREATEST THING IN THE WORLD

BY
HENRY DRUMMOND
(1851 – 1897)

INTRODUCTION

I was staying with a party of friends in a country house during my visit to England in 1884.[1] On Sunday evening as we sat around the fire, they asked me to read and expound some portion of Scripture. Being tired after the services of the day, I told them to ask Henry Drummond, who was one of the party. After some urging, he drew a small Testament from his hip pocket, opened it at the 13th chapter of I Corinthians, and began to speak on the subject of love.

It seemed to me that I had never heard anything so beautiful, and I determined not to rest until I brought Henry Drummond to Northfield[2] to deliver that address. Since then I have requested the principals of my schools to have it read before the students every year. The one great need in our Christian life is love, more love to God and to each other. Would that we could all move into Paul's chapter, and live there.

D. L. Moody

Love the LORD your God with all your heart and with all your soul and with all your strength. These commandments that I give to you today are to be upon your hearts. Impress them upon your children. Talk about them when you sit at home and when you walk along the road, when you lie down and when you get up.

Deuteronomy 6:5-7, NIV

1 CORINTHIANS 13, KJV

Though I speak with the tongues of men and of angels, and have not charity, I am become as sounding brass, or a tinkling cymbal.

And though I have the gift of prophecy, and understand all mysteries, and all knowledge; and though I have all faith, so that I could remove mountains, and have not charity, I am nothing.

And though I bestow all my goods to feed the poor, and though I give my body to be burned, and have not charity, it profiteth me nothing.

Charity suffereth long, and is kind; charity envieth not; charity vaunteth not itself, is not puffed up,

Doth not behave itself unseemly, seeketh not her own, is not easily provoked, thinketh no evil;

Rejoiceth not in iniquity, but rejoiceth in the truth;

Beareth all things, believeth all things, hopeth all things, endureth all things.

Charity never faileth: but whether there be prophecies, they shall fail; whether there be tongues, they shall cease; whether there be knowledge, it shall vanish away.

For we know in part, and we prophesy in part.

But when that which is perfect is come, then that which is in part shall be done away.

When I was a child, I spake as a child, I understood as a child, I thought as a child: but when I became a man, I put away childish things.

For now we see through a glass, darkly; but then face to face: now I know in part; but then shall I know even as also I am known.

And now abideth faith, hope, charity, these three; but the greatest of these is charity.

1

THE GREATEST IS LOVE

Everyone has pondered the great question of antiquity and of the modern world: "What is the *summum bonum*—the supreme good?" You have life before you. Once only can you live it. To live it to the highest degree possible, what is the noblest object of desire, the supreme gift to covet?

We have become accustomed to being told that the greatest thing in the religious world is faith. For centuries that great word has been the keynote of Christianity, and we have easily learned to look upon faith as the greatest thing in the world. Well, we are wrong. If we have been told that, we may miss the mark. In the 13th chapter of 1 Corinthians, Paul takes us to Christianity at its source, to its very root—and there we see, "The greatest of these is love."[3]

> *What is the supreme good?*

Paul's statement is not an oversight. He speaks of faith just a moment before. He says, "though I have all faith, so that I could remove mountains, but have not love, I am nothing."[4]

So far from forgetting, he deliberately contrasts them, "And now abide faith, hope, love, these three," and without a moment's hesitation his decision falls, "but the greatest of these is love."[5]

His statement is not prejudice either. People are apt to recommend to others their own strong point. Love was not Paul's strong point. The observing student can detect a beautiful tenderness growing and ripening all through his character as Paul gets older. But when we first meet the hand that wrote, "The greatest of these is love," it is stained with blood.

The supreme good is love.

Nor is Paul's letter to the Corinthians peculiar in singling out love as the *summum bonum*, the supreme good. The masterpieces of Christianity in the New Testament are agreed about it. Peter says, "And above all things have fervent love for one another."[6] Above all things. And John goes further, "God is love."[7]

You remember the profound remark that Paul makes elsewhere, "love is the fulfillment of the law."[8] Did you ever think what he meant by that? In those days, people were working the passage to heaven by keeping the Ten Commandments, and the many other commandments they had manufactured out of them. Then Jesus came and, in effect, said, "I will show you a more simple way. If you do one thing, you will do all these other things without ever thinking about them. If you love, you will unconsciously fulfill the whole law." Later, the Holy Spirit said the same thing through the apostle Paul.

Love is a simple way to fulfill the law.

You can readily see for yourselves how that must be so. Take any of the commandments. "Thou shalt have no other gods before me."[9] If we love God, no one has to tell is us that love is the fulfilling of that

8

law. Or "You shall not take the name of the LORD your God in vain."[10] Would we ever dream of taking His name in vain if we love Him? Or "remember the Sabbath day to keep it holy."[11] Would we not be too glad to have one day in seven to dedicate more exclusively to the object of our affections? Love, therefore, would fulfill all these laws regarding God.

It is the same with those who love people—you would never think of telling them to honor their fathers and mothers.[12] They could not do anything else. It would be preposterous to tell them not to kill.[13] And you would only insult them if you suggested that they should not steal[14]— how could they steal from those they loved? In the same way, it would be superfluous to ask them not to bear false witness against their neighbors.[15] If they loved them it would be the last thing they would do. And you would never dream of urging them not to covet what their neighbors had.[16] They would rather their neighbors possessed it than themselves. In this way, you see, "love is the fulfilling of the law." Indeed, it is the rule for fulfilling all rules, the new commandment for keeping all the old commandments—Jesus' one secret of the Christian life.

Now Paul has learned this, undoubtedly taught to him by the Holy Spirit, and in this noble eulogy he has given us the most wonderful and original account still in existence of the *summum bonum*. We may divide it into three parts. In the beginning of his short chapter we have love *contrasted*; in the heart of it, we have love *analyzed*; toward the end, we have love *defended* as the supreme gift.

> *Where there is love*
> *there is no need*
> *for law.*

9

2

LOVE CONTRASTED

Paul begins by contrasting love with other things that people in those days thought much of. I shall not attempt to go over these things in detail. Their inferiority is already obvious.

He first contrasts it with *eloquence*. And what a noble gift that is—the power of playing upon the souls and wills of people and rousing them to lofty purposes and holy deeds! Paul says, "Though I speak with the tongues of men and of angels, but have not love, I have become sounding brass or a clanging cymbal."[17] We all know why. We have all felt the brazenness of words without emotion—the hollowness and unaccountable unpersuasiveness of eloquence when there is no love behind it, nothing to give it force and power.

Then he contrasts it with *prophecy*. He contrasts it with *mysteries*. He contrasts it with *faith*. He contrasts it with *charity*. Why is

> The genius of Christianity is to have proclaimed that the path to the deepest mystery is the path of love.

love greater than faith? Because the end is greater than the means. Why is it greater than charity? Because the whole is greater than the part.

Love is greater than faith because the end is greater than the means. What is the purpose of having faith? It is to connect the soul with God. What is the object of connecting us with God? That we may become like God. But God is love. Thus the purpose of faith (the means) is so that we might love (the end). Love, therefore, is obviously greater than faith. "And though I have all faith, so that I could remove mountains, but have not love, I am nothing."[18]

Faith is greater than charity, again, because the whole is greater than a part. Charity, as Paul speaks of it in the first part of verse 3, is only a little bit of love, one of the innumerable avenues of love. But there may even be, and often is, a great deal of charity without love. It is a very easy thing to toss a coin to someone asking for money on the street; it is, in fact, generally an easier thing than not to do it. Yet love is just as often in the withholding. We purchase relief from the sympathetic feelings roused by the spectacle of misery, at the coin's cost. It is too cheap, too cheap for us, and often too dear for the person seeking help. If we really loved such persons we would either do more for them, or less. So Paul states, "And though I bestow all my goods to feed the poor, . . . but have not love, it profits me nothing."[19]

> "Ah Christ, that it were possible
> For one short hour to see
> The souls we loved,
> That they might tell us
> What and where they be."
> - Alfred, Lord Tennyson

Paul then contrasts love with sacrifice and martyrdom: "And though I give my body to be burned, but have not love, it profits me nothing."[20] Missionaries can take nothing greater to the non-Christian world than the impression and reflection of God's love upon their own characters. That is the universal language. It will often take them years to learn to speak a foreign language, and so they most often have to speak through interpreters. But from the day they land, the language of God's divine love, which is understood by all, will be pouring forth its unconscious eloquence.

It is the people who are the missionaries, it is not their words. Their character is their message. In the heart of Africa, among the great Lakes, I have come across native men and women who remembered the only white man they ever saw before—David Livingstone.[21] As you cross his footsteps in that dark continent, faces light up as they speak of the kind doctor who passed there years ago. They could not understand him, but they felt the love that beat in his heart. They knew that it was love, although he himself could speak few words in their language.

Take into your sphere of labor, where you also mean to lay down your life, the simple charm of love, and your lifework must succeed. You can take nothing greater, you need take nothing less. You may take every accomplishment, you may take every training and talent, you may be braced for every sacrifice, but if you give your body to be burned, and have not love, it will profit you and the cause of Christ nothing.

Lord, make me an instrument of Your peace. Where there is hatred let me sow love; where is injury, pardon; where there is doubt, faith; where there is despair, hope; where there is darkness, light; where there is sadness, joy. O divine Master, grant that I may not so much seek to be consoled as to console; to be understood as to understand; to be loved as to love. For it is in giving that we receive; it is in pardoning that we are pardoned; and it is in dying that we are born to eternal life.

Attributed to Saint Francis of Assisi

3

LOVE ANALYZED

After contrasting love, Paul, in three short verses, gives us an amazing analysis of what this supreme good, this *summum bonum*, is.

I ask you to look at it closely. It is a compound thing, he tells us. It is like a beam of light passing through a crystal prism and coming out the other side of the prism broken up into its component colors—red, blue, yellow, violet, orange, and all the colors of the rainbow. Paul, in effect, passes this thing called love through the magnificent prism of his Holy Spirit inspired intellect, and it comes out on the other side broken up into its elements.

> *Love is like a diamond comprised of nine perfect facets.*

In these few words we have what one might call the spectrum of love, the analysis of love. Will you observe what its elements are? Will you notice that they have common names; that they are virtues which we hear about every day; that they are things that can be practiced by every person in every place in life; and how, by a multitude of small things and ordinary virtues, the supreme thing, the *summum bonum*, is made up?

The spectrum of love has nine ingredients:

Patience . . . . Love is patient.

Kindness . . . . Love is kind.

Generosity . . . . Is not jealous.

Humility . . . . Love does not brag and is not arrogant.

Courtesy . . . . Does not act unbecomingly.

Unselfishness . . . . It does not seek its own.

Good temper . . . . Is not provoked.

Guilelessness . . . . Does not take into account a wrong suffered.

Sincerity . . . . Does not rejoice in unrighteousness, but rejoices with the truth.

"Love is patient, love is kind, and is not jealous; love does not brag and is not arrogant, does not act unbecomingly; it does not seek its own, is not provoked, does not take into account a wrong suffered, does not rejoice in unrighteousness, but rejoices with the truth."[22] Patience, kindness, generosity, humility, courtesy, unselfishness, good temper, guilelessness, sincerity—these make up the supreme gift, the stature of the perfect person.

> The angel that presided o'er my birth -
> Said "Little creature, formed of joy and mirth,
> Go love without the help of anything on earth."
> - William Blake

You will observe that all are in relation to people, in relation to life, in relation to the known today and the near tomorrow, and not to the unknown eternity. We hear much of love to God—Christ spoke much of love to people. We make a great deal of peace with heaven—Christ made much of peace on earth. Religion is not a strange or added thing, but the inspiration of the secular life, the breathing of the eternal Spirit through this temporal world. The supreme thing, in short, is not a thing at all, but the giving of a further finish to the multitudinous words and acts that make up the sum of every common day.

PATIENCE

This is the normal attitude of love—love passive, love waiting to begin, not in a hurry, calm, ready to do its work when the summons comes, but meantime wearing the ornament of a meek and quiet spirit. "Love is patient . . . bears all things, believes all things, hopes all things."[23] For love understands, and therefore waits.

KINDNESS

Love active. Have you ever noticed how much of Jesus' life was spent in doing kind things—in *merely* doing kind things? Read over the Gospels with that in view, and you will find that He spent a great proportion of His time simply in making people happy, in doing good turns to people. There is only one thing greater than happiness in the world, and that is holiness. Happiness is not in our keeping, but what God *has* put in our power is the happiness of those about us, and that is largely to be secured by our being kind to them.

> "Freely we serve,
> Because we freely love,
> as in our will
> To love or not;
> in this we
> stand or fall."
> -John Milton

Someone has said, "The greatest thing a person can do for our Heavenly Father is to be kind to some of His other children." I wonder why it is that we are not all kinder than we are? How much the world needs it! How easily it is done! How instantaneously it acts! How infallibly it is remembered! How superabundantly it pays itself back—for there is no debtor in the world so honorable, so superbly honorable, as love. "Love never fails."[24] Love is success, love is happiness, love is life. "Love," I say with Browning,[25] "is energy of life."

> For life, with all it yields of joy or woe
> And hope and fear,
> Is just our chance o' the prize of learning love, —
> How love might be, hath been indeed, and is.

Where love is, God is. They who abide in love abide in God.[26] God is love. Therefore, *love*. Without distinction, without calculation, without procrastination, *love*. Lavish it upon the poor, where it is very easy, and especially upon the rich, who often need it most. But most of all lavish love upon our equals, where it is very difficult, and for whom perhaps we each do least of all. There is a difference between *trying to please* and giving *pleasure*. Give pleasure. Lose no chance of giving pleasure, for that is the ceaseless and anonymous triumph of a truly loving spirit.

> Many waters cannot quench love, neither can the floods drown it.
> -Song of Songs 8:7a

I shall pass through this world but once. Any good thing, therefore, that I can do, or any kindness that I can show to any human being, let me do it now. Let me not defer it or neglect it, for I shall not pass this way again.[27]

GENEROSITY

"Love does not envy."[28] This is love in competition with others. Whenever you attempt a good work you will find others doing the same kind of work, and probably doing it better. Envy them not. Envy is a feeling of ill will to those who are in the same line as ourselves, a spirit of covetousness and detraction. Even Christian work is little protection against unchristian feelings. That most despicable of all the unworthy moods that cloud a Christian's soul assuredly waits for us on the threshold of every work, unless we are fortified with this grace of generosity. Only one thing truly needs the Christian envy—the large, rich, generous soul that "does not envy."

One word frees us of the weight and pain of life— that word is love.

HUMILITY

After having learned all that, you have to learn this further thing: humility—to put a seal upon your lips and forget what you have done. After you have been kind, after love has stolen forth into the world and done its beautiful work, go back into the shade again and say nothing about it. Love hides even from itself. Love waives even self-satisfaction. "Love does not parade itself, is not puffed up."[29] Humility is love hiding.

"There is but one road to lead to God—humility."
-Nicolas Boileau

COURTESY

The fifth ingredient is a somewhat strange one to find in this *summum bonum*: courtesy. This is love in society, love in relation to etiquette, love in relation to consideration for others. "Love does not behave itself rudely (unseemly, KJV)."[30]

Politeness has been defined as love in trifles. Courtesy is said to be love in little things. Consideration may be thought of as love in relationships. The secret of politeness, courtesy, and consideration is to love.

Love *cannot* behave itself rudely. You can put the most untutored persons into the highest society, and if they have a reservoir of love in their hearts they will not behave themselves rudely. They simply cannot do it. Carlyle[31] said of Robert Burns[32] that there was no truer gentleman in Europe than the ploughman-poet.[33] It was because he loved everything—the mouse and the daisy and all the things great and small that God had made. So with this simple passport he could mingle with any society and enter courts and palaces from his little cottage

| Love everything God has made. |

on the banks of the Ayr.[34]

You know the meaning of the word "gentleman." It means a gentle man—a man who does things gently, with love. That is the whole art and mystery of it. The gentle man cannot in the nature of things do an ungentle, an ungentle manly thing. The ungentle soul, the inconsiderate, unsympathetic nature, cannot do anything else. "Love does not behave itself rudely."

UNSELFISHNESS

"Love does not seek its own." Observe: *seeks not even that which is her own.* In Britain the people are devoted, and rightly, to their rights. It is the same in America. But there come times when we exercise even the higher right of giving up our rights.

Yet Paul does not summon us to give up our rights. Love strikes much deeper. It would have us not seek them at all, ignore them, eliminate the personal element altogether from our calculations.

It is not hard to give up our rights. They are often eternal. The difficult thing is to give up *ourselves.* The more difficult thing still is not to seek things for ourselves at all. After we have sought them, bought them, won them, deserved them, we have taken the cream off them for ourselves already. It's a small cross then to give them up. But not to seek them, to look not on our own things, but on the things of others—that is the difficulty.

> Love seeketh not itself to please,
> Nor for itself hath any care,
> But for another gives its ease,
> And builds a heaven in Hell's despair."
> - William Blake

"Do you seek great things for yourself?" said the prophet; "Do not seek them" Why? Because there is no greatness in *things*. Things cannot be great. The only greatness is unselfish love. Even self-denial in itself is nothing, and is almost a mistake. Only a great purpose or a mightier love can justify the waste.

It is more difficult, I have said, not to seek our own at all than having sought it to give it up. I must take that back. It is only true of a partly selfish heart. Nothing is a hardship to love, and nothing is hard. Christ's "yoke" is easy. Christ's yoke is just His way of our having true life. It is an easier way than any other. It is a happier way than any other. The most obvious lesson in

> It is more blessed to give than to receive.
> - Acts 20:35b

Christ's teaching is that there is no happiness in having and getting anything, but only in giving. I repeat—*there is no happiness in having or in getting, but only in giving.* Half the world is on the wrong scent in pursuit of happiness. They think it consists in having and getting, and in being served by others. It consists in giving, and in serving others. "Anyone who wants be great among you," said Jesus, "must be your servant."[35] If you would be happy, remember that there is but one way: "It is more blessed, it is more happy, to give than to receive."[36]

GOOD TEMPER

The next ingredient is a remarkable one: "love is not provoked." Nothing could be more striking than to find this here. We are inclined to look upon bad temper as a harmless weakness. We speak of it as a mere infirmity of nature, a family failing, a matter of temperament, not a thing to take into serious

> "If religion has done nothing for your temper, then it has done nothing for your soul."
> -James B. Clayton

account in estimating a person's character. Yet, right here in the heart of Paul's analysis of love, it finds a place—and the Bible again and again returns to condemn a bad temper as one of the most destructive elements in human nature.

The peculiarity of ill temper is that it is the vice of the virtuous. It is often the one blot on an otherwise noble character. You know men who are all but perfect, and women who would be entirely perfect, but for an easily ruffled, quick-tempered, or "touchy" disposition. This compatibility of ill temper with high moral character is one of the strangest and saddest problems of ethics. The truth is, there are two great classes of sins—sins of the *body* and sins of the *disposition*.

The Prodigal Son may be taken as a type of the first, the Elder Brother of the second.[37] Now, society has no doubt whatever as to which of these is the worse. Its brand falls, without a challenge, upon the Prodigal. But are we right? We have no balance to weigh one another's sins, and *coarser* and *finer* are but human words. Faults in the higher nature may appear to us less wicked than those in the lower, but to the eye of Him who is love, a sin against love may seem a hundred times more base.

No form of vice, not worldliness, not greed of gold, not drunkenness itself, does more to un-Christianize society

22

than evil temper. For embittering life, for breaking up communities, for destroying the most sacred relationships, for devastating homes, for withering up men and women, for taking the bloom of childhood; in short, for sheer misery-producing power, this influence stands alone.

Look at the Elder Brother—moral, hard working, patient, dutiful. Give him get all credit for his virtues, and yet look at this man, this baby, sulking outside his own father's door. "He was angry," we read, "and would not go in."[38] Look at the effect upon the father, upon the servants, upon the happiness of the guests. Judge the effect upon the Prodigal, and ask yourself how many prodigals are kept out of the kingdom of God by the unlovely character of those who profess to be inside. Analyze, as a study in temper, the thunder-cloud itself as it gathers upon the Elder Brother's brow.

> "Too often we have just enough religion to make us hate but not enough to make us love one another."
>
> -Jonathan Swift

What is the thunder-cloud made of? Jealousy, anger, pride, stinginess, cruelty, self-righteousness, touchiness, doggedness, sullenness—these are the ingredients of this dark and loveless soul. In varying proportions, also, these are the ingredients of all ill temper. Judge if such sins of the disposition are not worse to live in, and for others to live with, than the sins of the body.

Indeed, did Christ not answer this question Himself when He said, "Verily I say unto you that the publicans and the harlots go into the kingdom of God before you"?[39] There is really no place in heaven for a disposition like this. A person with such a mood could only make heaven miserable for all the people in it. Except, therefore, such a person is born again, that person cannot, simply cannot, enter the kingdom of heaven.[40] You will see then why temper is significant. It is not in what it is alone, but in what it reveals.

This is why I speak of it with such unusual plainness. It is a test for love, a symptom, a revelation of an unloving nature at the bottom. It is the intermittent fever that bespeaks intermittent disease within; the occasional bubble escaping to the surface that betrays some rottenness underneath; a sample of the most hidden products of the soul dropped involuntarily when off one's guard; in a word, the lightning form of a hundred hideous and un-Christian sins. A want of patience, a want of kindness, a want of generosity, a want of courtesy, a want of unselfishness, are all instantaneously symbolized in one flash of temper.

> Where there is love, there is no anger; where there is anger, there is no love.

Hence it is not enough to deal with the temper. We must go to the source and change the inmost nature, and the angry moods will die away of themselves. Souls are made sweet not by taking the acid fluids out, but by putting something in—a great love, a new spirit, the Spirit of Christ. Christ, the Spirit of Christ, interpenetrating ours, sweetens, purifies, transforms all. This only can eradicate what is wrong, work a chemical change, renovate and regenerate, and rehabilitate the inner person. Willpower does not change people. Time does not change people. Christ does. Therefore, "Let this mind be in you, which was also in Christ Jesus."[41]

> It is better not to live than not to love.

Some of us have not much time to lose. Remember, once more, that this is a matter of life or death. I cannot help speaking urgently for myself—and for you. "Whosoever shall offend one of these little ones that believe in me, it is better for him that a millstone were hanged about his neck,

24

and he were cast into the sea."[42] That is to say, it is the deliberate verdict of the Lord Jesus that it is better not to live than not to love.

> Love comforts like sunshine after rain.

GUILELESSNESS

Guilelessness is the grace for suspicious people who are always looking for evil in others. The possession of guilelessness is the great secret of personal influence. You will find, if you think for a moment, that the people who influence you are people who believe in you and think the best of you—even with all your faults. In an atmosphere of suspicion people shrivel up. But in an open atmosphere of acceptance and belief, they expand and find encouragement and enlightening fellowship.

It is a wonderful thing that here and there in this hard, uncharitable, world there should still be left a few rare souls who think no evil. This is the great unworldliness, that which is not of this world. Love "thinks no evil,"[43] imputes no motive, sees the bright side, puts the best construction on every action, What a delightful state of mind to live in! What a stimulus and benediction even to meet with it for a day! To be trusted is to be saved. If we try to influence or elevate others, we shall soon see that success is in proportion to their belief of our belief in them. The respect of others is the first restoration of the self-respect they have lost. Our ideal of what people are becomes to them the hope and pattern of what they may become.

> Love truth,
> but
> pardon error.

SINCERITY

"Love rejoiceth not in unrighteousness, but rejoiceth with the truth."[44] I have called this sincerity, from the words rendered in the Authorized Version (KJV) by "rejoiceth *in*

25

the truth." And, certainly, were this the real translation, nothing could be more just—for those who love will love truth not less than people. If we love, we will rejoice in the truth—rejoice not in what we have been taught to believe, not in this or that church's doctrine, not in this ism or in that ism, but "in *the truth*." We will accept only what is real. We will strive to get at facts. We will search for *truth* with humble and unbiased minds, and cherish whatever we find at any sacrifice.

The more literal translation of the Revised Version calls for just such a sacrifice for *truth's sake* here. For what Paul really meant is, as we there read, "Rejoiceth not in unrighteousness, but rejoiceth *with* the truth," a quality which probably no one English word—and certainly not sincerity—adequately defines. It includes, perhaps more strictly, the self-restraint that refuses to make capital out of others' faults; the charity that delights not in exposing the weakness of others, but "covereth all things";[45] the sincerity of purpose that endeavors to see things as they are, and rejoices to find them better than suspicion feared or calumny denounced.

> Hatred stirs up dissension, but love covers all wrongs.
> -Proverbs 10:12, NIV

✱✱✱

So much for the analysis of love. Now the business of our lives is to have these things fitted into our characters. That is the supreme work to which we need to address ourselves in this world, to learn love. Is life not full of opportunities for learning love? Every man and woman every day has a thousand of them. The world is not a playground, it is a schoolroom. Life is not a holiday, but an education. The one eternal lesson for us all is *how better we can love.*

What makes a person a good cricketer?[46] Practice. What makes a person a good artist, a good sculptor, a good musician? Practice. What makes a person a good linguist, a good stenographer? Practice. What makes a person a good person? Practice. Nothing else. There is nothing capricious about religion. We do not get the soul in different ways, under different laws, from those in which we get the body and the mind. If you do not exercise your body you cannot develop strong muscles, and if you do not exercise your soul, you acquire no muscle in your soul, no strength of character, no vigor of moral fiber, no beauty of spiritual growth. Love is not a thing of enthusiastic emotion. It is a rich, strong, vigorous expression of the whole round Christian character—the Christlike nature in its fullest development. The constituents of this great character are only to be built up by ceaseless practice.

> Let those love now who never loved before. Let those who always loved, now love the more.

What was Christ doing in the carpenter's shop? Practicing. Though perfect, we read that *He* learned obedience, and grew in wisdom and in favor with God. Do not quarrel, therefore, with your lot in life. Do not complain of its never-ceasing cares, its petty environment, the vexations you have to stand, the small and sordid souls you have to live and work with. Above all, do not resent temptation, and do not be perplexed because it seems to thicken round you more and more, and ceases neither through effort, agony, or prayer. That is your practice. That is the practice that God appoints you—and it is having its work in making you patient, humble, generous, unselfish, kind, and courteous. Do not grudge the hand that is molding the still too shapeless image within you. That image is growing more beautiful, though you see it not, and every touch of temptation may add to its perfection. Therefore stay in the middle of life. Do not isolate yourself. Be among people and things, among troubles and difficulties, among obstacles.

You remember Goethe's words: "Talent develops itself in solitude; character in the stream of life."[47] Talent develops itself in solitude—the talent of prayer, of faith, of meditation, of seeing the unseen. Character grows in the stream of the world's life, in the midst of the world's torrent. That chiefly is where we are to learn love.

> Love cannot be created, it can only be learned.

Now, how are we to love? To make it easier, I have named a few of the elements of love. But these are only elements. Love itself can never be defined. Light is something more than the sum of its ingredients—a glowing, dazzling, tremulous ether.[48] Love also is something more than the sum of its elements—a palpitating, quivering, sensitive, living thing. By synthesis of all the colors, scientists can create whiteness, but they cannot create light. By synthesis of all the virtues, we can create virtue, but we cannot create love.

How then are we to have this transcendent living thing conveyed into our souls? We brace our wills to secure it. We try to copy those who have it. We lay down rules about it. We watch. We pray. But these things alone will not bring love into our nature. Love is an *effect*. Only as we fulfill the right condition can we have the effect produced. Shall I tell you what the *cause* is?

If you turn to the Revised Version of the First Epistle of John you find these words: "We love because he first loved us."[49] "We love," not "We love him." That is the way

---

"Goodness and love mold the form into their own image, and cause the joy and beauty of love to shine forth from every part of the face. When this form of love is seen it appears ineffably beautiful, and affects the inmost life of the soul."

-Emanuel Swedenborg

the old version (KJV) has it,[50] and it is quite wrong. "We love—because he first loved us." Look at that word "because." It is the *cause* of which I have spoken. "*Because* he first loved us*," the effect follows that we love—we love Him, we love all people. We cannot help it. Because He loved us, we love—we love everybody. Our heart is slowly changed.

Contemplate the love of Christ, and you will love. Stand before that mirror, reflect Christ's character, and you will be changed into the same image from tenderness to tenderness. There is no other way. You cannot love to order. You can only look at the lovely object, and fall in love with it, and grow into likeness to it. And so look at this Perfect Character, this Perfect Life. Look at the great sacrifice as He laid down Himself, all through life, and upon the Cross of Calvary, and you must love Him. Loving Him, you most become like Him. Love begets love. It is a process of induction. Put a piece of iron in the presence of an electrified body, and that piece of iron for a time becomes electrified. It is changed into a temporary magnet in the mere presence of a permanent magnet, and as long as you leave the two side by side, they are both magnets alike.[51] Remain side by side with Him who loved us, and gave Himself for us, and you, too, will become a permanent magnet, a permanently attractive force. Like Him you will draw everyone to you, and like Him you will be drawn to everyone. That is the inevitable effect of love. Christians who fulfill that cause must have that effect produced in them.

Try to give up the idea that religion comes to us by chance, or by mystery, or by caprice. It comes to us by natural law, or by supernatural law, for all law is Divine.

> "*Love is He,*
> *radiant with great splendor,*
> *And speaks to us of thee,*
> *O Most High.*"
> -*St. Francis of Assisi*

Edward Irving went to see a dying boy once, and when he entered the room he just put his hand on the sufferer's head, and said, "My boy, God loves you," and went away. The boy started from his bed, and called out to the people in the house, "God loves me! God loves me!"

One word! It changed that boy. The sense that God loved him overpowered him, melted him down, and began the creating of a new heart in him. That is how the love of God melts down the unlovely heart in a person, and begets in that person the new creature, who is patient and humble and gentle and unselfish. There is no other way to get it. There is no mystery about it. We love others, we love everybody, we love our enemies, *because He first loved us.*

> *"Love for God is like the sun, which, as we journey toward it, casts the shadow of our burden behind us."*
> *-From a saying by Samuel Smiles*

How do I love Thee?
Let me count the ways.
I love thee to the depth and breadth and height
My soul can reach, when feeling out of sight
For the ends of Being and ideal Grace.
I love thee with the breath,
Smiles, tears, of all my life! — and if God choose
I shall but love thee better after death.

-Elizabeth Barrett Browning

4

LOVE DEFENDED

Now I have a closing sentence or two to add about Paul's reason for singling out love as the supreme possession.

It is a very remarkable reason. In a single word it is this: *it lasts*. "Love," urges Paul, "never fails."[52] Then he begins again one of his marvelous lists of the great things of the day, and exposes them one by one. He runs over the things that people thought were going to last, and shows that they are all fleeting, temporary, passing away.

> *"They sin who tell us love can die;*
> *With life all other passions fly,*
> *All others are but vanity."*
> -Robert Southey

"Whether there are prophecies, they will fail."[53] It was the mother's ambition for her boy in those days that he should become a prophet. For hundreds of years God had never spoken by means of any prophet, and at that time the prophet was greater than the king. People waited wistfully for another messenger to come, and hung upon his lips when he appeared, as upon the very voice of God. Paul says,

"Whether there are prophecies, they will fail." The Bible is full of prophecies. One by one they have "failed." That is, having been fulfilled, their work is finished, and they have nothing more to do now in the world except to feed a devout person's faith.

Then Paul talks about *tongues*. That was another thing that was greatly coveted. "Whether there are tongues, they will cease."[54] As we all know, many, many centuries have passed since tongues have been known in this world. They have ceased.[55] Take it in any sense you like. Take it, for illustration merely, as languages in general—a sense which was not in Paul's mind at all, and which though it cannot give us the specific lesson, will point the general truth. Consider the words in which these chapters were written—Greek. It has gone.[56] Take the Latin, the other great tongue of those days. It ceased long ago.[57] The language of Wales, of Ireland, of the Scottish Highlands is dying before our eyes.

Prophesies will finish their work.

Languages will vanish.

The most popular book in the English tongue at the present time (1884), except the Bible, is one of Dickens' works, his *Pickwick Papers*.[58] It is largely written in the language of London street-life, and experts assure us that in fifty years it will be unintelligible to the average English reader.

Then Paul goes further, and with even greater boldness adds "Whether there is knowledge, it will vanish away." The wisdom of the ancients, where is it? It is wholly gone. A schoolchild today knows more than Sir Isaac Newton knew; his knowledge has vanished away. You put yesterday's newspaper in the fire: its knowledge has vanished away. You can buy old editions of the great encyclopedias for a few dollars; their knowledge has vanished away. Look how the coach has been superseded by the use of steam, and how electricity has superseded that, and swept hundreds of almost new inventions into oblivion. "Whether there is knowledge, it shall vanish away." At every city workshop you will see, in the back yard, a heap of old 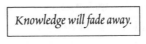 iron, a few wheels, a few *Knowledge will fade away.* levers, a few cranks, broken and eaten with rust. Machines that twenty years ago were the pride of the city, that people flocked in from the country to see as great invention, are now gone, superseded by better machines. All the boasted science and philosophy of this day will soon be old.

In my time at the University of Edinburgh, the greatest figure in the faculty was Sir James Simpson, the discoverer of chloroform.[59] Recently his successor and nephew, Professor Simpson, was asked by the librarian of the university to go to the library and pick out the books on his subject (midwifery)[60] that were no longer needed. His reply to the librarian was this: "Take every textbook that is more than ten years old and put it down in the cellar."

Sir James Simpson was a great authority only a few years ago, doctors went to Edinburgh from all parts of the world to consult him, and yet almost the whole teaching of his time is consigned by the science of today to oblivion. In every branch of science it is the same. "For we know in part," Paul said.[61] Knowledge does not last.

Can you tell me anything that is going to last? Many things Paul did not condescend to name. He did not mention money, fortune, or fame. But he picked *Nothing of the world will last.* out the great things of his time, the things that most people thought had something in them, and brushed them peremptorily aside. Paul had no charge against these things in themselves. All he said about them was that they would not last. They were great things, but not supreme things. There were things beyond them.

33

What we are, stretches past what we do, and beyond what we possess. Many things that people denounce as sins are not sins—they are just temporary and of no value. That is a favorite argument of the New Testament. John speaks of the world not as wrong, but simply that it "is passing away."[62] There is a great deal in the world that is delightful and beautiful, there is a great deal in it that is great and engrossing, but it will not last. All that is in the world, "the lust of the flesh, the lust of the eyes, and the pride of life,"[63] are but for a little while. "Do not love the world or the things in the world"[64] Nothing that it contains is worth the life and consecration of an immortal soul. The immortal soul must give itself to something that is immortal. The only immortal things are these: "Now abide faith, hope, love, . . . but the greatest of these is love."[65]

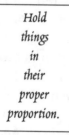

Hold things in their proper proportion.

Some think the time may come when two of these three things will also pass away—faith into sight, hope into fruition. Paul does not say so. We know but little now about the conditions of the life that is to come. But what is certain is that love must last. God, the Eternal God, is love.

Covet, therefore, that everlasting gift, that one thing that it is certain is going to stand, that one coinage that will be current in the universe when all the other coinages of all the nations of the world will be useless and unhonored. You will give yourselves to many things—give yourself *first* to love. Hold things in their proportion. Let at least the first great object of our lives be to achieve the character defended in these words, the character—and it is the character of Christ—that is built around love.

I have said this thing is eternal. Did you ever notice how continually John associates love and faith with eternal life? I was not told when I was a boy that "God so loved the world that He gave His only begotten Son, that whoever believes in Him should not perish but have everlasting life."[66] What I was told, I remember, was that God so loved the world that, if I trusted in Him, I was to have a thing called peace, or I was to have rest, or I was to have joy, or I was to have safety. But I had to find out for myself that whosoever trusted in Him—that is, whosoever loved Him, for trust is only the avenue to love—has everlasting life.

The gospel offers a person a life. Never offer people a thimbleful of gospel. Do not offer them merely joy, or merely peace, or merely rest, or merely safety. Tell them how Christ came to give everyone a more abundant life than they have—a life abundant in [God's] love, and therefore abundant in salvation for themselves, and large in enterprise for the alleviation and redemption of the world. Then only can the gospel take hold of the whole of a person, body, soul and spirit, and give to each part of the person's nature its exercise and reward.

Many of the current gospels are addressed only to a part of a person's nature. They offer peace, not life; faith, not love; justification, not regeneration. People slip back again from such religion because it has never really held them. Their nature was not all in it. It offered no deeper and gladder life-current than the life that was lived before. Surely it stands to reason that only a fuller love can compete with the love of the world.

"They that love beyond the world cannot be separated by it. Death is but crossing the world, as friends do the seas; they live in one another still."

-William Penn

To love abundantly is to live abundantly, and to love forever is to live forever. Hence, eternal life is inextricably bound up with love. We want to live

"Love not pleasure, love God."
-Thomas Carlyle

forever for the same reason that we want to live tomorrow. Why do we want to live tomorrow? Is it because there is someone who loves you, and whom you want to see tomorrow, and be with, and love back? There is no other reason why we should live on than that we love and are beloved. It is when people have no one to love them that they commit suicide. So long as they have friends, those who love them and whom they love, they will live, because to live is to love. Be it but the love of a dog, it will keep a person in life. But let that go, and a person has no contact with life, no reason to live. That's why so many today die by their own hands.

Eternal life also is to know God, and God is love. This is Christ's own definition. Ponder it. "This is eternal life, that they may know You, the only true God, and Jesus Christ whom You have sent."[67] Love *must* be eternal. *It is what God is.*

There is only one happiness in life,
to love and be loved.

In the last analysis, then, love is life. Love never fails, and life never fails—so long as there is love. That is the philosophy of what Paul is showing us. It is the reason why in the nature of things love should be the supreme thing— because it is going to last, and because in the nature of things it is an eternal life. It is a thing that we are living now, not that we get when we die. Indeed, we shall have a poor chance of getting it when we die unless we are living it now. No worse fate can befall a person in this world than to live and grow old alone, unloving and unloved. To be lost is to live in an unregenerate condition, loveless and unloved. To be saved is to love—to love is to be saved. They who abide in love abide already in God—for God is love.[68]

Now I have all but finished. Will you join me in reading 1 Corinthians 13 once a week for the next three months? A man did that once and it changed his whole life. Will you do it? It is for the greatest thing in the world.

> Everything in the world can be endured except a life without love.

You might begin by reading it every day, especially the verses that describe the perfect character. "Love suffers long and is kind; love does not envy; love does not parade itself, is not puffed up." Get these ingredients into your life. Then everything that you do is eternal. It is worth doing. It is worth giving time to. You cannot become a saint in your sleep. To fulfill the condition required, demands a certain amount of prayer, meditation, and time, just as improvement in any direction, bodily or mental, requires preparation and care. Address yourself to that one thing, and at any cost have this transcendent character exchanged for your present one.

You will find as you look back upon your life that the moments that stand out, the moments when you have really lived, are the moments when you have done things in a spirit of love. As memory scans the past, above and beyond all the transitory pleasures of life, there leap forward those supreme hours when you have been enabled to do unnoticed kindnesses to those round about you, things too trifling to speak about, but which you feel have entered into your eternal life.

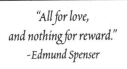

> "All for love,
> and nothing for reward."
> -Edmund Spenser

I have seen almost all the beautiful things God has made. I have enjoyed almost every pleasure that He planned for humanity. Yet as I look back, I see standing out above all the life that has gone four or five short experiences when the love of God reflected itself in some poor imitation, some small act of love of mine, and these seem to be the things that alone of all one's life abide. Everything else in all our lives is transitory. Every other good is visionary. But the acts of love that no person knows about, or can ever know about, they never fail.

In the Book of Matthew, where the Judgment Day is depicted for us in the imagery of One seated upon a throne and dividing the sheep from the goats, the test of a person then is not, "How have I believed?"

> Nothing in all creation is so like God as love.
> -From a saying by Meister

but "How have I loved?" The test of religion, the final test of religion, is not religiousness, but love. I say again, the final test of religion at that great Day is not religiousness, but love. Not what I have done, not what I have believed, not what I have achieved, but how I have discharged the common charities of life. Sins of commission in that awful indictment are not even referred to. By what we have not done, by sins of omission, the omission of love, we are judged. It could not be otherwise.

The withholding of love is the *negation* of the Spirit of Christ, the proof that we never knew Him, that for us He lived in vain. It means that He suggested nothing in all our thoughts, that He inspired *nothing in* all our lives, that we were not once near enough to Him to be seized with the spell of His compassion for the world. It means that—

> I lived for myself, I thought for myself,
>
> For myself, and none beside—
>
> Just as if Jesus had never lived,
>
> As if He had never died.

38

It is the Son of Man before whom the nations of the world will be gathered. It is in the presence of humanity that we will be charged. The spectacle itself, the mere sight of it, will silently judge each one. Those will be there whom we have met and helped—or there, the unpitied multitude whom we neglected or despised. No other witness

Because of deep love, one is courageous before God.

need be summoned. No other charge than love withheld shall be preferred. Be not deceived. The words that all of us shall one day hear sound not of theology but of life, not of churches and saints but of the hungry and the poor, not of creeds and doctrines but of shelter and clothing, not of Bibles and prayer books but of cups of cold water in the name of Christ.

Thank God the Christianity of today is coming nearer the world's need. Live and love to help that on.

Thank God people know better, by a hair's breadth, what religion is, what God is, who Christ is, where Christ is.

Who is Christ? He who fed the hungry, clothed the naked, visited the sick.

Where is Christ? "Whoever receives one of these little children in My name receives Me."[69]

Who are Christ's? "Everyone who loves is born of God and knows God."[70]

"Only where the heart is can the true treasure be found."
-James Matthew Barrie

39

ENDNOTES TO SECTION 1

1 Mr. Moody had two extended mission trips to Great Britain—the first from 1873 to 1875, the second from 1881 to 1884.

2 The Moody family had lived in Northfield, Massachusetts, since the beginning of the 19th century, and there Mr. Moody established his permanent home on 12 acres that he purchased near his mother's home in 1875. In 1878, he purchased 100 acres with a "pleasing view of the Connecticut Valley," and there built the Northfield Seminary for Women. It was formally opened on November 3, 1879. The first classes were held in Mr. Moody's dining room until the recitation hall was completed in January. Twenty years later Mr. Moody purchased 275 acres of land overlooking the Connecticut River and built the Mount Hermon School for Young Men, naming it after the reference to Hermon in Psalm 133:3. Mount Hermon is also considered to be the traditional site of Jesus' transfiguration. Thousands flocked every summer to the Northfield Bible Conferences at the Seminary, and Moody brought the best Bible teachers from around the world to teach at the conferences and the schools. Moody died at his home in Northfield on December 22, 1899, and is buried near his house on a green knoll known as "Round Top."

[3] 1 Corinthians 13:13b
[4] 1 Corinthians 13:2
[5] 1 Corinthians 13:13
[6] 1 Peter 4:8
[7] 1 John 4:8
[8] Romans 13:10
[9] Exodus 20:3
[10] Exodus 20:7
[11] Exodus 20:8
[12] Exodus 20:12
[13] Exodus 20:13
[14] Exodus 20:15

[15] Exodus 20:16
[16] Exodus 20:17
[17] 1 Corinthians 13:1
[18] 1 Corinthians 13:2b
[19] 1 Corinthians 13:3
[20] 1 Corinthians 13:3b
[21] David Livingstone (1813-1873) worked in Africa as a medical missionary and traveled the continent from the equator to the Cape and from the Atlantic to the Indian Ocean. Responding to an appeal in 1834 by British and American churches for medical missionaries to go to China, he decided this should be his career and spent the next two years working part-time and studying theology and medicine. But he was prevented from going to China by the Opium War. Later he met Robert Moffat, a noted missionary to southern Africa, who convinced him that he should take up his work in Africa.

Livingstone arrived in Cape Town, Africa, on March 14, 1841. Though he did not know it at the time, he would spend most of the rest of his life in Africa, doing missionary work and exploring the interior of the continent. The first European to travel so extensively into previously uncharted territory, Livingstone was determined to open up Africa to Christianity and Western commerce, to find the source of the Nile River, and, if possible, to destroy the slave trade. His first expedition lasted until 1849, when he returned to England to publish and lecture on his journey. On his second major expedition (1850-1856) he discovered and named Victoria Falls on the Zambezi on Nov. 17, 1855.

During his last expedition (1866-1873), Livingstone's lines of communication were broken, and for five years his exact whereabouts were unknown and he was presumed dead. An American reporter, Henry M. Stanley of the *New York Herald,* was given the assignment to "Go find Livingstone." Stanley found him on the shores of Lake Tanganyika, an ill and failing man. Stanley was so astounded to find Livingstone alive that all he could think to say was, "Dr. Livingstone, I presume?" With Stanley's supplies and help, Livingstone resolved to continue his quest for the Nile's source, but they did not succeed. Stanley returned to England in March 1872, but Livingstone would not return with him.

On May 1, 1873, Livingstone's servants found him dead in a village in what is now Zambia. His body was taken to England and buried in Westminster Abbey on April 18, 1874.

[22] 1 Corinthians 13:4-6

[23] 1 Corinthians 13:4, 7a

[24] 1 Corinthians 13:8

[25] Elizabeth Barrett Browning (1806-1861), renowned British poet. Her greatest work, *Sonnets from the Portuguese* (1850), is a sequence of love poems written to her husband.

[26] 1 John 4:16b

[27] Saying attributed to Stephen Grellet (Etienne de Grellet du Mabillier, 1773-1855), though it has not been found in his writings. Most commonly attributed as a proverbial saying by anonymous.

[28] 1 Corinthian 13:4

[29] ibid

[30] 1 Corinthians 13:5

[31] Several versions give the name as Carlisle, but the person quoted is probably Thomas Carlyle (1795-1881), British historian and essayist.

[32] Robert Burns (1759-1796) is considered to be Scotland's major poetic voice and greatest poet. His lyrics, written in dialect and infused with humor, celebrate love, patriotism, and rustic life.

[33] So called because he wrote much of his poetry while he was a farmer.

[34] Robert Burns's birthplace, on Firth of Clyde, 30 miles s.w. of Glasgow—now a summer resort.

[35] Matthew 20:26

[36] Acts 20:35

[37] Luke 15:1-32

[38] Luke 15:28

[39] Matthew 21:31, KJV

[40] John 3:3

[41] Philippians 2:5

[42] Mark 9:42

[43] 1 Corinthians 13:5

[44] 1 Corinthians 13:6, probably original Revised Standard Version (rarely published today)

[45] Proverbs 10:12, KJV

[46] Cricket is an outdoor game played with bats, a ball, and wickets by two teams of 11 players each; it is more than 300 years old, and is regarded as the English national sport.

[47] Actual quotation is: "A talent is formed in stillness, a character in the world's torrent." It is from *Torquato Tasso* [1790], act I, sc. ii, by Johann Wolfgang von Goethe (1749-1832)

[48] It was formerly thought that ether (physics) was the medium by which electromagnetic waves were spread.

[49] 1 John 4:19 Also translated this way in the *New Revised Standard Bible* and the *New American Standard Bible*, including the 1995 NASB edition.

[50] The *New King James Version, The New International Version*, and *The Living Bible* also translate it this way.

[51] This book was written in 1884 and the knowledge of electricity and magnetism was still in its infancy—Thomas Edison had installed the world's first central electric power plant in New York City just two years before.

[52] 1 Corinthians 13:8

[53] ibid

[54] ibid

[55] This was written before the Pentecostal outpouring around the world in the early 1900s and since that time.

[56] This refers to the Greek language that was spoken from about 800 B.C. to around A.D. 300.

[57] Latin ceased being an important cultural language about the end of the 17th century, but it is still used by certain ecclesiastical groups.

[58] The *Pickwick Papers* were a monthly serial that first appeared in England in April 1836, featuring a humorous character named Mr. Pickwick. The stories made Charles Dickens' (1812-1870) perhaps the most popular and best known English writer of that time. Today, of course, he is best known for *David Copperfield* and *A Christmas Carol*.

[59] Actually, Sir James Simpson (1811-1870) did not discover chloroform, it was discovered in Germany in 1831 and at almost the same time in France and the United States. Sir James Simpson

was a Scottish physician in Edinburgh who in 1847 pioneered the use of ether and chloroform in obstetrics. It was for this that he became famous.

[60] The techniques and practice of a midwife, a person, usually a woman, who is trained to assist women in childbirth.

[61] 1 Corinthians 13:9

[62] 1 John 2:17

[63] 1 John 2:16

[64] 1 John 2:15

[65] 1 Corinthians 13:13

[66] John 3:16

[67] John 17:3

[68] 1 John 4:16

[69] Mark 9:37

[70] 1 John 4:7

HENRY DRUMMOND

Henry Drummond was born in Sterling, Scotland, on August 7, 1851. He attended Edinburgh University, and though he never received a degree, he became an ordained minister and professor of theology, a lecturer in natural science in 1877 at the Free Church of Glasgow, and wrote several religious and scientific books. He was also a geologist and explorer and traveled often on scientific explorations. After making a geological survey of southern Africa, he wrote one of his most popular books, *Tropical Africa.* Another book, *The Ascent of Man,* was also well accepted.

Much of Drummond's Christian teachings and writings were an attempt to reconcile science and religion. He believed that the natural and spiritual realms were so close, that the natural laws that governed the growth and maturing of plants were essentially the same as the spiritual laws that governed the growth and maturing of the human soul. In 1883 his book, *Natural Law in the Spiritual World*, was published, sold 70,000 copies in five years, and made him famous.

None of his other teachings and books, however, gained the popularity or endurance of his small booklet, *The Greatest Thing in the World.* In the beginning, it was merely an exposition on 1 Corinthians 13 that Drummond occasionally gave. Then Dwight Moody heard the teaching in 1884 during his second extended mission to Great Britain, and the rest is history.

This is how it came about according to Mr. Moody's son, Will R. Moody:

At the close of the [London] mission, Mr. Moody accepted an invitation to spend a few days for rest and recreation at the country house of T. A. Denny, and later at the home of his brother, Edward Denny. With him were also invited a score or more of those who had assisted in the work in London, including among others, Professor Drummond, who had returned from his tour into the interior of Africa in time to be present during the closing weeks of the meetings. Those were delightful days for Mr. Moody, who, free from the care and strain of his great work, gave himself up to the relief of social life, enjoying particularly the young people's games.

During this period of rest, Mr. Moody made frequent attempts to draw from Drummond a little of the wealth of information that he possessed. This Drummond did on a beautiful Sunday afternoon in June, where they were together at the home of Mr. Edward Denny, not far from Tunbridge Wells, whence, thirteen years later, after months of painful suffering, Drummond entered upon his reward. In those days, however, he was at the zenith of physical strength, and stood before the Christian world as the suddenly famous author of *Natural Law in the Spiritual World.*

An urgent request was made of Mr. Moody to give an informal address. "No," was the response, "you've been hearing me for eight months, and I'm quite exhausted. Here's Drummond. He will give you a Bible reading."

With characteristic reluctance Drummond consented, and taking from his pocket a little Testament, he read the thirteenth chapter of First Corinthians. Then, without a note and in the most informal way, gave that exposition of Christian duty that has become so widely known to hundreds-of-thousands under the title of *The Greatest Thing in the World.*

Three years later, when visiting Northfield at Mr. Moody's request, the same exposition was repeated, both at the Students' Conference and the August Conference [Northfield Bible Conference held each summer]. Later, in response to Mr. Moody's urgent plea, it was published in its present booklet form. Mr. Moody often said that he wished this address to be read in the Northfield schools every year, and that it would be a good thing to have it read once a month in every church till it was known by heart.

Professor Drummond was only twenty-two when in 1873 he began his work with Mr. Moody in Scotland. When, in later years, the fires of criticism were kindled against Drummond, his great-hearted friend stood by him. He believed in the *man* with all his heart, even though he could not follow [agree with] him in all his *theories.* He knew him to be a Christian "who lived continually in the thirteenth chapter of First Corinthians." Is it a wonder that the affection between these two broad-minded, loving-hearted, men became a bond that could not be severed?

To those who knew both, it was not a matter of surprise that, speaking to Dr. Henry Clay Trumbull alone, at different times in the same day, each should say of the other, "He is the sweetest-tempered Christian I ever knew."

Henry Drummond died on March 11, 1897. Yet through this single small booklet he continues to live and influence generations of Christians to love God, to love their neighbors, and to love each other.

1 Corinthians 13

NASB

13:1 If I speak with the tongues of men and of angels, but do not have love, I have become a noisy gong or a clanging cymbal.

2 If I have the gift of prophecy, and know all mysteries and all knowledge; and if I have all faith, so as to remove mountains, but do not have love, I am nothing.

3 And if I give all my possessions to feed the poor, and if I surrender my body to be burned, but do not have love, it profits me nothing.

4 Love is patient, love is kind and is not jealous; love does not brag and is not arrogant,

5 does not act unbecomingly; it does not seek its own, is not provoked, does not take into account a wrong suffered,

6 does not rejoice in unrighteousness, but rejoices with the truth;

7 bears all things, believes all things, hopes all things, endures all things.

8 Love never fails; but if there are gifts of prophecy, they will be done away; if there are tongues, they will cease; if there is knowledge, it will be done away.

9 For we know in part and we prophesy in part;

10 but when the perfect comes, the partial will be done away.

11 When I was a child, I used to speak like a child, think like a child, reason like a child; when I became a man, I did away with childish things.

12 For now we see in a mirror dimly, but then face to face; now I know in part, but then I will know fully just as I also have been fully known.

13 But now faith, hope, love, abide these three; but the greatest of these is love.

NRSV

13:1 If I speak in the tongues of mortals and of angels, but do not have love, I am a noisy gong or a clanging cymbal.

2 And if I have prophetic powers, and understand all mysteries and all knowledge, and if I have all faith, so as to remove mountains, but do not have love, I am nothing.

3 If I give away all my possessions, and if I hand over my body so that I may boast, but do not have love, I gain nothing.

4 Love is patient; love is kind; love is not envious or boastful or arrogant

5 or rude. It does not insist on its own way; it is not irritable or resentful;

6 it does not rejoice in wrongdoing, but rejoices in the truth.

7 It bears all things, believes all things, hopes all things, endures all things.

8 Love never ends. But as for prophecies, they will come to an end; as for tongues, they will cease; as for knowledge, it will come to an end.

9 For we know only in part, and we prophesy only in part;

10 but when the complete comes, the partial will come to an end.

11 When I was a child, I spoke like a child, I thought like a child, I reasoned like a child; when I became an adult, I put an end to childish ways.

12 For now we see in a mirror, dimly, but then we will see face to face. Now I know only in part; then I will know fully, even as I have been fully known.

13 And now faith, hope, and love abide, these three; and the greatest of these is love.

1 CORINTHIANS 13

NKJV

13:1 Though I speak with the tongues of men and of angels, but have not love, I have become sounding brass or a clanging cymbal.

2 And though I have the gift of prophecy, and understand all mysteries and all knowledge, and though I have all faith, so that I could remove mountains, but have not love, I am nothing.

3 And though I bestow all my goods to feed the poor, and though I give my body to be burned, but have not love, it profits me nothing.

4 Love suffers long and is kind; love does not envy; love does not parade itself, is not puffed up;

5 does not behave rudely, does not seek its own, is not provoked, thinks no evil;

6 does not rejoice in iniquity, but rejoices in the truth;

7 bears all things, believes all things, hopes all things, endures all things.

8 Love never fails. But whether there are prophecies, they will fail; whether there are tongues, they will cease; whether there is knowledge, it will vanish away.

9 For we know in part and we prophesy in part.

10 But when that which is perfect has come, then that which is in part will be done away.

11 When I was a child, I spoke as a child, I understood as a child, I thought as a child; but when I became a man, I put away childish things.

12 For now we see in a mirror, dimly, but then face to face. Now I know in part, but then I shall know just as I also am known.

13 And now abide faith, hope, love, these three; but the greatest of these is love.

NIV

13:1 If I speak in the tongues of men and of angels, but have not love, I am only a resounding gong or a clanging cymbal.

2 If I have the gift of prophecy and can fathom all mysteries and all knowledge, and if I have a faith that can move mountains, but have not love, I am nothing.

3 If I give all I possess to the poor and surrender my body to the flames, but have not love, I gain nothing.

4 Love is patient, love is kind. It does not envy, it does not boast, it is not proud.

5 It is not rude, it is not self-seeking, it is not easily angered, it keeps no record of wrongs.

6 Love does not delight in evil but rejoices with the truth.

7 It always protects, always trusts, always hopes, always perseveres.

8 Love never fails. But where there are prophecies, they will cease; where there are tongues, they will be stilled; where there is knowledge, it will pass away.

9 For we know in part and we prophesy in part,

10 but when perfection comes, the imperfect disappears.

11 When I was a child, I talked like a child, I thought like a child, I reasoned like a child. When I became a man, I put childish ways behind me.

12 Now we see but a poor reflection as in a mirror; then we shall see face to face. Now I know in part; then I shall know fully, even as I am fully known.

13 And now these three remain: faith, hope and love. But the greatest of these is love.

SECTION 2

THE GREATEST THING IS LOVE

BY
HAROLD J. CHADWICK

INTRODUCTION

Over the 25 years of my Christianity, I have read Henry Drummond's exposition of 1 Corinthians 13 at least twice a year. Yet each time I finished it I felt that it was incomplete, that it was not wrapped up, if you will, and that there was something more that he should have said.

It took me some time to realize that that "something more" was an explanation of the type of love that the inspired apostle Paul was talking about. I realized, finally, that my sense of incompleteness was my personal inability to harmonize Paul's statements about what love was with the professed love I saw in Christianity and felt within myself. Both always came far short of Paul's analysis of love—so short, in fact, that they hardly seemed related.

Through those years I also learned two other things: I am unable to produce Paul's type of love within myself, and if just one of the elements is missing or imperfect, it is not the love that he meant. In other words, even if I have all the elements working, and only *patience* (long-suffering) is missing or less than it should be, it is not the love of 1 Corinthians 13—it is something other than that.

The nine elements comprise, or together make up, Paul's love, and not a single one of them can be missing or imperfect. It is sort of like a nine-faceted diamond with one of the facets damaged—the diamond is not perfect, it is something other than that. The love Paul wrote about is perfect love—and any missing or damaged element makes it a different type of love.

That being so, I realized that only God can love that way. So the type of love Paul wrote about had to be God's love—His love manifested in us and through us. That realization changed everything. I stopped struggling to love and started learning to receive God's love—or rather, perhaps, by faith to allow God's love that is already in me to manifest in me and through me.

However, like Paul said about himself in his letter to the Philippians, I haven't yet reached that state of perfect love—I am, indeed, far from it. I have simply learned to keep stretching upward like Paul for the high calling of God in Christ Jesus and let Him do the work in me. In doing so, I have found that it is much easier and much more effective God's way than my way.

In 1 Corinthians 13, the Greek word that is used for love is the noun *agape*. Jesus took this word, one of two ordinary Greek words for love, and elevated and redefined it as God's type of love—Divine love. He used it almost exclusively in his teachings about love, and Paul used it almost exclusively in his epistles. The other epistle writers, however, including the writer of the letter to the Hebrews, for some reason used the other Greek word for love, *phileo*, which means love in a social, moral sense—the love between friends. Perhaps like Peter in his discourse with Jesus as recorded in John 21, they had not yet learned the difference between the words or the types of love.

It may be that Paul received his understanding of love when he was taken up into Paradise,[1] which may have also been when he received his gospel: "the gospel I preached is not something that man made up. I did not receive it from any man, nor was I taught it; rather, I received it by revelation from Jesus Christ."[2] Whenever and wherever he learned about God's type of love, Paul and Jesus used the same Greek word to express it: *agape*.

So the purpose of this section that has been added to Henry Drummond's book is to define and explain God's type of love that Paul wrote about in 1 Corinthians 13. My explanation is not derived from any teaching about it in the New Testament, for there is no teaching about it. I puzzled over this for some time, considering the importance of our understanding it, and Jesus' and Paul's emphases on it.

Then it slowly dawned on me, as most things do, that Jesus would not have explained it for He explained almost nothing directly, and Paul probably taught and spoke of it often in person, and so there was no need to explain it in his letters. This is the reason why many things in the New Testament are not explained—they were common knowledge or, perhaps, the verbal teaching simply wasn't recorded. We have, for example, no recordings of the many teachings Paul did in person, such as his all-night teaching when he put Eutychus to sleep,[3] and less than 4000 words of all that Jesus spoke are recorded for us.

Now you may not agree with everything of the little that I understand and have written about *agape*, and that is well. Or your understanding of it may be much greater than mine, and that is better. There is also the possibility, of course, that I haven't explained it well. Nevertheless, though my flame may flicker dimly, perhaps someone may be able to light their candle from it. If so, that alone would make my attempt to explain the absolute wonder and glory of God's type of love in us and through us well worth the writing.

Harold J. Chadwick

1 CORINTHIANS 13, 14:1A, AMP

If I [can] speak with the tongues of men and [even] of angels, but have not love [that reasoning, intentional, spiritual devotion such as is inspired by God's love for and in us], I am only a noisy gong or a clanging cymbal.

And if I have prophetic powers—that is, the gift of interpreting the divine will and purpose; and understand all the secret truths and mysteries and possess all knowledge, and if I have (sufficient) faith so that I can move mountains, but have not love [God's love in me] I am nothing—a useless nobody.

Even if I dole out all that I have [to the poor in providing] food, and if I surrender my body to be burned [or in order that I may glory], but have not love [God's love in me], I gain nothing.

Love endures long and is patient and kind; love never is envious nor boils over with jealousy; is not boastful or vainglorious, does not display itself haughtily.

It is not conceited—arrogant and inflated with pride; it is not rude (unmannerly), and does not act unbecomingly. Love [God's love in us] does not insist on its own rights or its own way, for it is not self-seeking; it is not touchy or fretful or resentful; it takes no account of the evil done to it—pays no attention to a suffered wrong.

It does not rejoice at injustice and unrighteousness, but rejoices when right and truth prevail.

Love bears up under anything and everything that comes, is ever ready to believe the best of every person, its hopes are fadeless under all circumstances and it endures everything [without weakening].

Love never fails—never fades out or becomes obsolete or comes to an end.[4]

When I was a child, I talked like a child, I thought like a child, I reasoned like a child; now that I have become a man, I am done away with childish ways and have put them aside.[5]

And so faith, hope, love abide; [faith, conviction and belief respecting man's relation to God and divine things; hope, joyful and confident expectation or eternal salvation; love, true affection for God and man, growing out of God's love for and in us], these three, but the greatest of these is love.[6]

Eagerly pursue and seek to acquire [this] love—make it your aim, your great quest.

5

WHAT IS LOVE?

Love, the apostle Paul says, is the greatest thing in the world—it even surpasses faith, without which we cannot please God,[7] and hope, which is the anchor of our soul that enters within the veil.[8] Without love, Paul asserts, anything that we do for God or people is worthless, and all our natural abilities and even the Holy Spirit's gifts are without value and profit us nothing. Everything that exists in this age will fail and pass away, he says, except love—it alone will not fail and will last eternally.

In the light of this astounding revelation by the Holy Spirit through the apostle Paul, it is essential to our Christianity that we understand clearly what this unfailing love is, why it is the greatest thing in the world, and how we can obtain

> Divine love is the glorious discovery of Christianity.
> -From a saying by William Ellery Channing.

it and manifest it in our lives. If it is impossible to please God without faith, and we cannot enter into eternal life without hope, and love is greater than both of these, then love must be, as Henry Drummond stated, the greatest or supreme good in this age—and in the next, for love is eternal.

Throughout the ages of humanity, the greatest or supreme good—the *summum bonum*—that philosophers have searched for is "a final or ultimate value of conduct that is desirable in itself and not merely the means to an end." Though few of the philosophers throughout time found it or agreed upon what it is, the Word of God clearly tells us: *The ultimate value of (unselfish) conduct that is desirable in itself is LOVE.*

The philosophical question of what it is and the scriptural answer are shown in a recorded incident in the New Testament. One day a lawyer (scribe) came to Jesus, testing Him, and asked:

"Teacher, which is the great commandment in the law?"

Jesus said to him, " 'You shall love the LORD your God with all your heart, with all your soul, and with all your mind.'

"This is the first and great commandment."[9]

The Lord had quoted out of the Book of Deuteronomy (6:5), and then He did a strange thing, something that had never been done before. He reached into the Book of Leviticus (19:18) and brought forth part of another verse and put it with the first and great commandment, literally making them a unit.

> Love is the telescope through which one sees far into God.

"And the second is like it: 'You shall love your neighbor as yourself.'

"On these two commandments hang all the Law and the Prophets."

The Lord also did something else. For *love* in both commandments He used an ordinary word for love that He had previously elevated to mean a divine type of love, God's love—as He used it in John 3:16: "For God so loved the world that He gave His only begotten Son, that whoever believes in Him should not perish but have everlasting life."

The Greek words for this divine type of love are the verb *agapao* and its corresponding noun *agape*. In addition to these words, there are two other Greek words in the New Testament that are used for love—they are the verb *phileo* and it's corresponding noun *philanthropia*,[10] from which we get the English noun *philanthropy*. But in New Testament usage there is a world of difference between the love expressed by these words. It's a difference that we must know if we are to comprehend Paul's famous dissertation on love, and know the unique form of that love as well as we can know it.

AGAPE AND PHILEO

In general, the words *agape* and *phileo* are used to speak of the two different types of New Testament love, and it is these words that we will use in this chapter.

The essence or basic nature of the two kinds of love is that *agape* is self-sacrificing love that benefits someone other than the person expressing the love, and *phileo* is self-satisfying love that benefits the person expressing the love.

Agape is a decision of the intellect and will, and *phileo* is a decision of the emotions. *Agape* does not depend upon feelings to benefit another, while *phileo* requires affection to do so. *Agape* does not consider the worthiness or unworthiness of the one it is benefiting, while *phileo* considers both. The inherent nature of *agape* is

> Love is what God is.

61

that it wholly considers the benefit of its recipient, while the inherent nature of *phileo* is that it considers the benefit of both its giver and its recipient, with the weight of benefit on the side of the recipient. In this we might say that *agape* is a do-good love and *phileo* is a feel-good love—*agape* is self-giving and *phileo* is a self-receiving. The difference in the two types of love is derived from their sources—*agape* is from God, *phileo* is from us. *Agape* is God's perfect love—*phileo* is our imperfect love.

The sacrificing, self-giving, nature of *agape* can be seen in the first eight words of John 3:16—

> *We pardon to the extent that we love.*

"God so loved the world that He gave . . ." The word here used for "loved" is the verb *agapao*, meaning, of course, that God's love for the world was expressed in His action of giving—and what God gave was obviously a self-sacrifice for Him. It would be in keeping with the nature of *agape* to say that you cannot express such love without sacrificing something of yourself.

Agape cannot be expressed with words, it can only be expressed with actions. This is a most important point, and one of the most difficult for us to learn and to practice.

In the Old Covenant, God only once expressed His love for His people by telling them directly that He loved them.[11] Instead, He expressed His love by His actions toward them. It is the same toward us in the New Covenant. God does not tell us with words that He loves us—"God *demonstrates* His own love toward us, in that while we were still sinners, Christ died for us" (Romans 5:8, italics for emphasis).

Similarly, Jesus never expressed His love for His disciples or us by His words. He never once said "I love you" to anyone of His time or to us. Instead, He expressed His love by dying for them and us on Calvary. We do not know that He loves us because of what He said, but because of what He did: "Christ also has loved us and given Himself for us, an offering and a sacrifice to God for a sweet-smelling aroma" (Ephesians 5:2).

If God had not given His Son for us, and that Son had not died for us, we would have no way of knowing that either of them truly loved us. It is because of what they did for us, not because of what they said to us, that we know that they love us.

> It isn't life that matters—it's the love you bring to it.
> -From a saying by Hugh Walpole

Ten thousand times ten thousand words expressing love have no meaning if there is not corresponding, self-sacrificing action. When Jesus gave His disciples what is now known as the third love commandment, "love [agape] one another as I have loved [agapao] you," He specified the essence of that love by telling them: "Greater love [agape] has no one than this, than to lay down one's life for his friends" (John 15:12-13). It is this love, agape, that the apostle Paul said is the greatest of all.

Unfortunately, in Christianity today it's the phileo form of love that predominates and that is assumed to be fulfilling the love commandments. But phileo is a love most often expressed with words and not with self-giving actions. It's a love based upon some level of affection because of the perceived worthiness of the one who is loved. If the perceived worthiness is removed, however, the affection soon disappears and so does the love. The love disappears because loving the unworthy

> To be able to say how much you love is to love but little.

without affection does not produce pleasure, and pleasure or some level of satisfaction must be produced in the one expressing the phileo form of love or it cannot sustain—for it is a self-satisfying love, not a self-sacrificing love.

Not many years ago, two internationally famous Christian evangelists who had been mightily used by God and ministered to millions all over the world fell from grace within a short time of each other. Hundreds of thousands had attended their meetings, been helped spirit, soul, and body by them, supported their ministries, prayed for them, and expressed continually in one way or another to them and to others how much they loved them. They were admired and loved by millions of Christians—or so the millions said.

Then they stumbled and fell.

When they did, the living and powerful Word of God cut like a two-edged sword between the souls and spirits of those millions and discerned the thoughts and intents of their hearts and whether the love they had so often expressed was *agape* or *phileo*. In the vast majority of those millions it was *phileo*, even in the hearts of those who later muttered pious words about how we *"have* to love our brothers."

> "Love is the stepping stone to new beginnings."
> - Thomas Kinkade

Agape doesn't *have* to be told to love, it doesn't know anything else to do—indeed, it is incapable of doing anything else. It is only *phileo* that has to be told to love, to try to find something worthy to love in the now unlovable, and to once more express some level of affection—even if it's only condescending.

Not understanding the difference between the two kinds of love, however, is not of recent origin in the Church, it has existed since Jesus first taught about this new kind of love, this divine way of loving, this self-sacrificing way of loving. The Scriptures show that not even Jesus' chosen disciples understood what their Master had taught them about it, which was not unusual for them, for until the descent of the Holy Spirit at Pentecost they had trouble with most of what He taught them. We have an example of the disciples' problems with understanding *agape* in John's gospel.

JESUS AND PETER

> So when they had eaten breakfast, Jesus said to Simon Peter, "Simon, son of Jonah, do you love Me more than these?" He said to Him, "Yes, Lord; You know that I love You." He said to him, "Feed My lambs."
>
> He said to him again a second time, "Simon, son of Jonah, do you love Me?" He said to Him, "Yes, Lord; You know that I love You." He said to him, "Tend My sheep."
>
> He said to him the third time, "Simon, son of Jonah, do you love Me?" Peter was grieved because He said to him the third time, "Do you love Me?" And he said to Him, "Lord, You know all things; You know that I love You." Jesus said to him, "Feed My sheep.[12]

Three times Jesus asked Peter if he loved Him. The first two times He used the verb *agapao*. By using the verb He was undoubtedly asking Peter if he loved Him in a willful, dynamic, and self-sacrificing way. But Peter replied by using the word *phileo*, meaning that he had strong affection for the Lord—loved Him in a social, moral, way. He obviously did not understand the difference between the words or the difference between the two types of love.

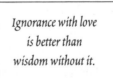

Ignorance with love is better than wisdom without it.

The last time Jesus asked Peter if he loved Him, He used the same word that Peter had used, *phileo*. In so doing, He dropped His love requirement down to the best that Peter could do at that stage of his spiritual development. Still not understanding, Peter was grieved because the Lord had asked Him a third time.

> *The path of love*
> *and the path of insight*
> *lead into the same garden.*
> *-Stephen Mittchell*

In all this there was undoubtedly a connection back to Peter's denying three times that He knew Jesus.[13] The Lord was now trying to show Peter that if he had loved Him with *agape*, he would have sacrificed whatever was necessary rather than deny knowing Him.

In the next verse, Jesus then told Peter what true love for Christ (*agape*) would cost him once he learned to walk in it:

"Most assuredly, I say to you, when you were younger, you girded yourself and walked where you wished; but when you are old, you will stretch out your hands, and another will gird you and carry you where you do not wish."

This He spoke, signifying by what death he would glorify God. And when He had spoken this, He said to him, "Follow Me."[14]

As Peter's love for Jesus Christ matured over the years, so did his spiritual understanding of the sacrificial nature of *agape*. In *The New Foxe's Book of Martyrs* (Bridge-Logos Publishers, Pure Gold Classics), we used an ancient story about Peter that well illustrates this point.

The only account that we have of the martyrdom of the apostle Peter is from the early Christian writer Hegesippus. His account includes a miraculous appearance by Christ. It seems that when Peter was old (John 21:18), Nero planned to put him to death. When the disciples heard of this, they begged Peter to flee the city [said to be Rome], which he did after much pleading by the disciples. But when he got to the city gate, he saw Christ walking toward him. Peter fell to his knees and said, "Lord, where are you going?" Christ answered, "I've come to be crucified again." By this, Peter understood that it was his time to suffer the death by which Jesus had told him he would glorify God (John 21:19), so he went back into the city. After being captured and taken to his place of martyrdom, he requested that he be crucified in an upside down position because he did not consider himself worthy to be crucified in the same position as his Lord.

If this story is true, or only partially true, it shows that in his later years Peter had greatly matured in his spiritual character and understanding, and had put away the childish ways that the twelve disciples so often exhibited when Jesus walked with them on the earth and taught them about the ways of God.

The King of love my Shepherd is,
Whose goodness faileth never;
I nothing lack if I am His,
And He is mine forever.

-Sir Henry William Baker

6

PUT AWAY CHILDISH THINGS

When I was a child, I spoke as a child, I understood as a child, I thought as a child; but when I became a man, I put away childish things. (1 Corinthian 13:11)

In the above statement, Paul is saying that when he physically matured and became a man, became an adult, he did not continue in childish ways but spoke as an adult, understood as an adult, thought as an adult. Having physically, mentally, and emotionally matured, he did not continue to think, understand, speak, or act as a child—he changed his ways to those of an adult.

In using this physical example of his growth to maturity, Paul is stating that we should similarly grow in

> It is well to think well;
> it is divine to love well.
> -From a saying by Horace Mann

our spiritual development—grow from being spiritual children to being spiritual adults. Our thoughts, understanding, and actions are no longer to be those of "babes in Christ,"[15] but of "those who are of full age, who by reason of use have their senses exercised."[16] We are to leave spiritual childhood and "go on to maturity."[17]

Now, it is easy to say that, but what is God's way for us to reach the maturity He desires for us?

NOT BY SELF-DISCIPLINE

It is not by way of trying to develop our spiritual character by self-discipline—taking one of our sins at a time and working at it until we have overcome it. That method only leads to self-congratulations, to self-aggrandizement, that increases our spiritual pride in our accomplishments. Too soon we arrive at self-made pinnacles from which we look down on others who have not reached the spiritual heights that we have, but who we know could if they would only do what we did. Self cannot improve self, it can only add more of the same—even if it calls the increase by a different name.

NOT BY HOPE

It is not by hope, for hope will have fruition in its own time, and that time will not be until the end of this age. Hope was not given to us by God to mature us, it was given "as an anchor for the soul, firm and secure. It enters the inner sanctuary behind the curtain, where Jesus, who went before us, has entered on our behalf."[18]

> "The simple heart that freely asks in love, obtains."
> -John G. Whittier

NOT BY FAITH

It is not by faith, even though "without faith it is impossible to please God."[19] Faith brings forth many wonderful things in this life, and it is a gift of God's grace whereby we might be saved.[20] But faith does not bring forth spiritual maturity, not even "mountain-moving faith."[21] Paul's first letter to the Church at Corinth speaks of their having all the gifts of the Holy Spirit in operation, including the gifts of healings and miracles, yet it was the most carnal of all the churches that he wrote to.

In this century we have all seen or heard of those who claim to exercise one or several gifts of the Holy Spirit, and those who seem to have the faith to perform miracles of healings. Yet in far too many of them we also see signs of spiritual immaturity: self-centeredness, self-esteem, self-exaltation, covetousness, greediness, competitiveness, love of power, love of fame, love of money—selling what God has freely given them rather than giving it freely.[22] This seeming paradox can be confusing unless we understand that spiritual gifts and mountain-moving faith do not necessarily denote spiritual maturity, and learn to discern the difference. Indeed, such gifts and faith, and even such things as true spiritual visions, can bring with them the great danger of exaltation—both by self and by others.

Even the inspired apostle Paul who wrote the love chapter, later wrote about how early in his apostleship "he was caught up into Paradise and heard inexpressible words, which it is not lawful for a man to utter."[23] But with the revelations came the danger of exaltation, and so: "lest I should be exalted above measure by the abundance of the revelations, a thorn in the flesh was given to me, . . . lest I be exalted above measure."[24]

> It is because God loves us that He does not answer many of our prayers.

NOT BY CHARITY

The way to spiritual maturity is not by charity either. Though we may tithe to the church we attend and give to many good works, and even work to help the poor, the downtrodden, or the ill, none of these add to our spiritual maturity. In fact, most of those who are involved in the latter works do not profess faith in Christ, and many do not even profess belief in God. If such things led to spiritual maturity, then all who did them would come to know God and Christ. There are many reasons for doing such works, even many good reasons, but as a way to spiritual maturity is not one of them, for it is not God's way.

ONLY ONE WAY

God has given us but one way to the spiritual maturity that He desires for each of us in this age, that we might be prepared for the work that He has *already* designated for us in the ages to come. That way is LOVE—and only LOVE. Neither self-discipline, hope, faith, nor charity changes our spiritual character, only love does. Love changes the heart, and it is from the heart that character springs. Thoughts of good or evil are formed within our hearts, and the thoughts of our hearts determine our actions.[25]

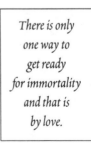

There is only one way to get ready for immortality and that is by love.

Therefore, the condition of your heart determines the spiritual condition of your character. As your heart is increasingly filled with and controlled by divine love, by God's type of love (*agape*), your spiritual character increasingly matures. There is no other way. Only self-giving, self-sacrificing love matures a Christian.

Since this is so, it should be easy for us to understand that it was for the purpose of spiritually maturing us that the Lord encompassed ALL our relationships—to God, to humanity, to each other—with three LOVE commandments:

Thou shalt love the Lord thy God with all thy heart, and with all thy soul, and with all thy mind.[26]

Thou shalt love thy neighbour as thyself.[27]

Love one another, as I have loved you.[28]

Now a person who has spiritually matured through love (*agape*) may have gifts of the Holy Spirit, may have mountain-moving faith, and may do many good works. But such a person will not speak of having gifts, nor speak of having mountain-moving faith—or some special anointing, nor speak of their good works. For one of the first elements of such love is true humility; and those

> *"The three greatest virtues of Christianity are: humility, humility, humility."*
> -St. Augustine

who are truly humble do not simply think of themselves as less, they do not think of themselves at all.

"Put away childish things"[29]—put away all things that have not to do with love and that are not born out of love. For love is God's only way to spiritual maturity. It is for this reason that Paul tells us to "pursue love."[30]

HOME AT LAST

Who seeks heaven alone to save his soul
May keep the path, but will not reach the goal;
He who walks in love may wander far,
Yet God will bring him where the blessed are.
                                    -Henry Van Dyke

7

PURSUE LOVE

Pursue love, and desire spiritual gifts, but especially that you may prophesy.[31]

Here is a direct command from God through Jesus Christ by the Holy Spirit[32] through the inspired pen of the apostle Paul: "Pursue love"—pursue *agape*. Not pursue spiritual gifts, not pursue faith, not pursue hope, not pursue charity, not pursue power, not pursue miracles—not pursue most, if not all, of the things that we now pursue in Christianity. These things we should *desire*, even as Paul stipulated about spiritual gifts and prophesy in our text-verse—but we are not to *pursue* them. It is only love that we are to pursue.

> *You have not fulfilled every duty, unless you have fulfilled that of love.*
> *-From a saying by Charles Burton*

The word *pursue* means: to follow in an effort to overtake or capture; to chase; to strive to gain or accomplish; to proceed along the course of a fixed goal. All of these meanings are included in Paul's admonition to pursue love.

The reason we are commanded to "pursue love" is obvious. In New Testament Christianity we are under three love commandments. Jesus said that on the first "two commandments hang all the law and the prophets."[33] In similar fashion, the apostle Paul wrote: "For all the law is fulfilled in one word, even in this: 'You shall love your neighbor as yourself.'"[34] So God has given us a single focus, a single goal, a single path to walk whereby we might fulfill ALL His laws and come into total agreement with Him in all things.

Considering this, what is it that God is working in us so that we will be willing to do those things that please Him?[35] It can be only one thing: love—*agape*. Thus we are admonished to work out, manifest outwardly, with fear and trembling, the love aspect of our salvation that God is working inwardly—that is,

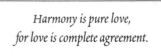

Harmony is pure love, for love is complete agreement.

within us.[36] For only love fulfills all the law, brings us into complete agreement with God, and enables us to live a life that is totally pleasing to Him.

Further, if love is the greatest or supreme good throughout the universe, and if it will never end but will last eternally, then it stands to reason that the pursuit of love has both temporal and eternally benefits and purposes. To spend time in pursuit of any good that is less than the supreme good is a waste of our spiritual energies, a disdaining of that which God has told us to pursue, and a direct disobedience of His command. To do so is to also spend our lives in the futile pursuit of those things that are only temporary.

In addition, when we leave this world, we will leave behind not only all material possessions, but also any gifts of the Holy Spirit that we might have been given, for they shall not be needed;

> *If I can touch the life of one person with true love, then I feel I shall have worked with God.*

all faith, for we shall see all things clearly; all hope, for it shall be realized; all charitable works, for there shall be none to be accomplished. All that we will take with is the love—divine eternal love—that we have pursued and obtained while we were here. If there were to be one supreme question to be asked us when we arrive at our eternal home, it would not be, "What did you accomplish?" but "How much did you love?"

"God is love,"[37] and as such He is, with all due reverence, like a great magnet that is drawn to love and draws love to itself. He is not impressed by our spiritual powers, for they are to Him who is all power like baby's toys. Neither is He impressed by our knowledge, for He possesses all knowledge and knows the beginning from the end. God is drawn to love, as is His Son: "he who loves Me will be loved by My Father, and I will love him and manifest [disclose, show] Myself to him."[38] Those who live in love, God draws to Himself and encloses them within Himself, so that those who live in love live in God Himself: "God is love. Whoever lives in love lives in God, and God in him."[39] There is no more secure place to dwell in all God's creation than in God Himself—and that secure place is acquired only by love.

In Christianity today, many things are sought after, and many things are held forth as the things to seek. Their merits and benefits are sounded far and wide and call to all who are searching for that element in their Christianity that

> *Love is the only investment that never fails.*
> *- From a saying by Henry David Thoreau*

they know is missing, though they do not know what it is. For this reason, many Christians constantly pursue whatever seems to be new, to be exciting, to be in vogue, to be "what the Holy Spirit is doing today." You have but to think of the thousands of meetings and conferences that are held each year all over the Christian world to know the truth of this. Yet few of the meetings and conferences concern the one thing that God has told us to pursue—love, divine love, God's type of love, *agape.*

Perhaps that is because *agape* is not self-gratifying or self-exalting—it does not outwardly benefit the one who loves, it benefits the one who is loved. It is also not something in which there can be the mass participation that creates excitement and a good time. Rather it is a quiet inward spiritual growth that in our heart decreases us and increases God, our Lord, and others. ""He must increase, but I must decrease."[40] "In humility consider others better than yourselves."[41]

> *A contented heart is the greatest blessing a person can enjoy in this life.*
> *-From a saying by Joseph Addison*

This humility is something that obviously developed in the apostle Paul as he walked further into Christ, and further into love. Whereas in his early letters he twice bragged about himself, though he said in one letter that he was a fool for doing so,[42] in one of his last letters, written when an old man in prison, he wrote: "I am less than the least of all God's people."[43]

Paul also exhibited another *agape* trait in his prison epistles: contentment. In his letter to the Philippians, written while in a prison cell in Rome, he wrote: "I have learned to be content whatever the circumstances."[44] Only a heart of love is a contented heart, for it has no disagreement with God, with itself, with it's neighbors, or with its circumstances—past, present, or future. A heart of love is a heart that is totally at peace.

Though we may not have yet reached Paul's heart condition, we can be encouraged by the first three words of his statement: "I have learned." It is recorded for our understanding and encouragement that Jesus learned obedience[45] and Paul learned love and its resulting contentment. As they learned, so can we.

God has two dwellings: one in heaven and the other in a meek and loving heart.

-From a saying by Isaac Walton

God's way to spiritual maturity is not an easy path to follow, or an easy one to stay upon, for the path up to the high things of God travels down most of the way. It is not a path that *self* desires to follow, and so it fights every step of the journey. But to "lay hold of that for which Christ Jesus has also laid hold of us," we must forget the things that are behind, forget self and the self-gratifying form of love (*phileo*), and "press toward the goal for the prize of the upward call of God in Christ Jesus."[46]

When we do, we will find that somewhere along the path, the Lord will meet us with such an overflow of divine love that it will be impossible for us to ever again love any other way than God's way.

NEIGHBOR

Love your neighbor for God's sake, and God for your own sake, who created all things for your sake, and redeemed you for His mercy's sake. If your love hath any other motive, it is false love. If you neglect your love to your neighbor, in vain you profess love of God; for by your love of God, your love to your neighbor is acquired; and by your love to your neighbor, your love of God is nourished.

-The Beauties of Thought

79

8

HOW THEN SHOULD WE LOVE?

Agape is the highest type of love that God could and has given us. "God has poured out His love [*agape*] into our hearts by the Holy Spirit."[47] He has *poured out* of Himself *agape* into our hearts that we might manifest an abundance of it in this life, and carry that abundance with us in our souls into the next life. But in far too many of us, *agape* lies dormant in our hearts, buried under a weight of carnal desires and attitudes, and substituted for by *phileo*, which we too often express with free abandonment and just as freely abandon when the object of this self-gratifying love no longer gratifies us.

Yet there is hope on the horizon, for God continues to work in our hearts to will and to do for His good pleasure,[48] — increasingly so as we draw closer to the time of our departure. Throughout the Church there are growing sounds of dissatisfaction with today's Christian life, and increasing signs of God's saints turning their eyes and hearts upward to God's higher ground.

> Love is but the name for the effect whose cause is God.

Lord lift me up and let me stand,
By faith on heaven's table land;
A higher plane than I have found,
Lord, plant my feet on higher ground.

I want to live above the world,
Tho Satan's darts at me are hurled;
For faith has caught the joyful sound,
The song of saints on higher ground.

The saints on higher ground are those who have learned to live and love for the benefit of others and have done away with concern of any benefits for themselves. To love with *agape* is to be willing to sacrifice *all things*—possessions and self—for the benefit of the one who is loved—regardless of the character or worthiness of the one who is loved, and regardless of difficult and changing circumstances and situations.

> Love is being willing to say, "I'm sorry."

When we have more than we can eat
To feed a stranger's not a feat.
When we have more than we can spend
It isn't hard to give or lend.
Who give but what they'll never miss
Will never know what giving is.
They'll win few praises from their Lord
Who do but what they can afford.
The widow's mite to heaven went
Because real sacrifice is meant.

God loves you regardless of how unlovable you may be today, and today He will steadfastly continue to work all things together for your good.[49] He does this not because of the wonderful person you are every moment of your life, but because of His unchangeable love for you. Nothing you say or do can change God's love for you, for God's love, like God Himself, is immutable—it neither varies to the right or left and there is no shadow of turning to it.[50] It is in this same way, if we love with *agape*, that we will love God and Christ, love our neighbors, and love each other—for it is God's *agape* that has been poured into our hearts to enable us to so love.

Those who give love to others cannot keep from receiving it themselves.

It is a blemish upon the Body of Christ that the divorce rate within the Church is as high as it is within the world. The problem lies in that the vast majority of Christian couples marry for *phileo* and not for *agape*. Like those in the world, they marry because they are emotionally and physically attracted to the other person, and because they believe that the other person will make them happy—in other words, they marry for self-gratification. Rarely does a Christian couple marry for *agape*, because they believe they can make the other person happy. Just as rarely is there sufficient *agape* in a *phileo* marriage to make it the kind of Christian marriage that God intends it to be. Yet *agape* is the solution to *all the difficulties* in Christian marriages, and the solution to the problem of the divorce rate within the Church.

It is also the solution to all the other problems in the Church, and in any local church. Name the problem: bickering, fighting, gossiping, covetousness, greediness, selfishness, divisions, lying, cheating, lusting,—put a thousand names to them, it doesn't matter, *agape* is the solution to them all. God in His wisdom has given us ONE solution for ALL problems—and we in our wisdom seek a different solution for every problem. Yet God's Word contains many examples and teachings to show us that we

> *Mrs. Browning, the poet, said to Charles Kingsley, the novelist,*
> *"What is the secret of your life? Tell me, that I may make mine more*
> *beautiful."*
> *Thinking for a moment, the beloved old author replied,*
> *"I had someone who loved me."*

should determine the conduct of our lives by love, just as life itself contains many examples for us.

In his book, *In the Face of Surrender*,[51] Richard Wurmbrand has many examples of the *agape* type of love. Here is one about Mayer Amshel Rothschild, founder of the Rothschild dynasty.

Mayer Amshel Rothschild, had been a poor boy who served in the house of Rabbi David Moshe of Chortkov. This rabbi had set aside in a drawer 200 golden coins as a dowry for his daughter. Rothschild married a girl from a nearby town and opened a little shop that did quite well.

A few years passed, and the time came for the rabbi's daughter to marry. As the wedding approached, the rabbi opened the drawer to take out the coins to give to the bridegroom, only to discover to his horror that the money was not there. No one in the house had any explanation as to how it could have disappeared. The suspicion fell on Rothschild. They asked themselves: *Where did he get the money to open his shop?* Surely he was the thief.

The rabbi defended him: "It is not right to accuse anyone without proof."

But the family insisted, "You must go and speak to him. Otherwise we will be disgraced. The guests will arrive soon, and the wedding will not take place."

Reluctantly the rabbi went, apologized for having to ask such an embarrassing question, but explained the terrible predicament in which he found himself. Looking his former employee in the eye he asked, "Do you know something about the money?"

Rothschild was silent a few minutes, then said, "I have stolen it. I will repay it here and now. Please forgive me."

The rabbi, who had an understanding for human sin, gladly forgave him. The wedding took place, and he officiated with great joy. For Rothschild, however, life became difficult. As others heard what he had done, he went broke and had to close his shop.

Several months later it was discovered that the 200 gold coins had been stolen by a servant girl, who shared it with a lover. At a drunken party the lover bragged how he came to possess the money. He was arrested, and both acknowledged their theft. The rabbi went to Rothschild and asked him pointedly, "Why did you confess to a sin you had not committed? And why did you give me the money?"

> Love in its simplest definition is merely a heart turned toward God.
> -From a saying by Phillips Brooks

He replied, "I saw you terribly sad. I imagined the weeping of your wife and of the girl. I was ready to give you all my money immediately to make up for the loss, but I knew you would not accept such a sacrifice from me. So I had to say I had stolen your money. Thus you were peaceful and had joy."

Then Rabbi Moshe returned the 200 gold coins to Rothschild and blessed him: "May God reward this deed of yours by giving you and all your descendants great riches." The blessing was fulfilled. The Rothschilds and their descendants became some of the richest people in the world.

Rothschild, of course, was not a Christian, yet he demonstrated the God type of love that Jesus defined and called *agape*. This type of love existed long before Jesus taught about it and gave it a name. Even as tithing and faith predated Old Covenant law and New Covenant grace, so

> The place of love, like that of God,
> is everywhere.
> -From a saying by John Quales

agape predated the time of Jesus. We have many stories in the Old Testament that show this, such as the story about Abram (Abraham) and Lot.

When there was strife between Abram's herdsmen and Lot's herdsmen because there wasn't enough land for all the livestock, Abram said to Lot: "Please let there be no strife between you and me, and between my herdsmen and your herdsmen; for we are brethren. Is not the whole land before you? Please separate from me. If you take the left, then I will go to the right; or, if you go to the right, then I will go to the left."[52]

Abram put himself in second place and put Lot's benefit before his. He would let Lot choose where he wanted to go, and he would take what was left. Lot, however, did not have the same love toward his uncle that Abram had toward him, and he put his own benefit before that of Abram. "Lot lifted his eyes and saw all the plain of Jordan, that it was well watered everywhere . . . Then Lot chose for himself all the plain of Jordan, and Lot journeyed east. And they separated from each other."[53]

Lot established his home in Sodom, where he should not have lived, and later he and all his household were taken captive when four kings raided Sodom and Gomorrah.

> A religion without love is a
> religion without God.

When Abram heard about it, he immediately "armed his three hundred and eighteen trained servants who were born in his own house, and went in pursuit." [54] There was no hesitation on Abram's part, no consideration of danger to himself and his servants. Lot was in trouble, Lot needed his help, and so he gathered all that he had and immediately went to help him.

After he had defeated the kings and returned Lot and his household to Sodom, the king of Sodom tried to reward him, but he refused, saying, "I have raised my hand to the LORD, God Most High, the Possessor of heaven and earth, that I will take nothing, . . . lest you should say, 'I have made Abram rich'"[55] Whatever rewards, whatever benefits, that Abram would receive for his actions, he would receive from God alone and from no one else. In all things, God must receive the glory. In all of this, Abram

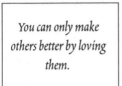

You can only make others better by loving them.

demonstrated love (*agape*) toward Lot and love (*agape*) toward God. Whether Lot ever learned to reciprocate this type of love is not known, for no further associate between Abram and Lot are recorded. But *agape* does not concern itself with reciprocation, it only concerns itself with benefiting the one it loves. It loves because it is its nature to love.

Here is another story of *agape* from *In the Face of Surrender*—it's from the Chuen-Chin period of Chinese history (15th B.C.):

> Tso-Po-Tao went on a journey with Yang-Chao-Ai, during which they were overtaken by a heavy snowstorm. Unprepared for this, they had neither the clothing nor the food to survive. Tso-Po-Tao offered to undress and give all his clothing and food to Yang-Chao-Ai so that he at least might be saved. Yang refused, but in vain. Tso was already naked and half-frozen. Tso died, and Yang's life was spared.

Note how exactly this story fits Jesus' statement about *agape*: "Greater love has no one than this, that he lay down his life for his friends."[56] Again, this love was manifested by someone who obviously was not a Christian, for the sacrifice of his life for his friend occurred 1500 years before

Jesus was born. has placed His hearts of all His like many things, 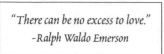 Perhaps God love in the creatures and, it was only brought out into the light and defined for us when His Son came to the earth to reveal His Father. If that is so, what a wonderful world this would be if only all of us could learn to live in that love!

In *The New Foxe's Book of Martyrs*[57] there are numerous stories about saints with love so great for God and Christ that not even the terror and pain of unspeakable torture and burning at the stake could turn them from it. In Richard Wurmbrand's book, *In the Face of Surrender,* there are similar stories about prisoners who sacrificed food, comfort, and even their lives for love of others. Both books should be studied carefully for a deeper understand of how we should love.

In the New Testament, Jesus gave us the parable of the *Good Samaritan* to help us to understand, and the story of the *Prodigal Son.* This latter story is most often viewed from the standpoint of the wasteful son who returns home, but Jesus intended it to be viewed from the standpoint of the father, for the parable demonstrates the love of our Father in heaven toward the wayward, and the way in which we also should love them.

"I think that to have known one good, old man—one man who through the chances and mischances of life, has carried his heart in his hand, like a palm-branch, waving all discords into peace—helps our faith in God, in ourselves, and in each other more than many sermons."

-George Wallace Curtis

Then we have Jesus Himself, his entire life and his sacrifice on Calvary. Throughout it all He demonstrated His love for His Father, and His love and God's love for us. No life has ever demonstrated it better in words and deeds. It is the force of that love that has been the power behind Christianity for 2000 years. Without that love there is no Christianity. Indeed, it is the lack of His *agape* type of love that has weakened today's Christianity as a force for godliness and good in this world.

Read the stories of the well-known and not-so-well-known saints of God down through the history of the Church, and you will find that the common denominator in all of their lives is love. In all of them, love is the source of their dedication to God and Christ, their godliness, and the good that they did. To name only a few, not in chronological order: St. Augustine, Francis of Assisi, Madame Jeanne Guyon, Fenelon, Julian of Norwich, John Hyde, George Mueller, Fanny Crosby, Sadhu Sundar Singh, St. John of the Cross, Brother Lawrence, John Bunyan, Thomas á Kempis, Howell Harris, Robert Murray McCheyne, David Brainerd, John Wycliffe, John Huss, William Booth, Hudson Taylor, Amy Carmichael, Mother Teresa. The list stretches from here into eternity.

Many of us desire to do great things for God, but the greatest thing we can do for Him is to learn to love as He loves. It is as Mother Teresa said:

"We can do no great things; only small things with great love."

Love is swift, sincere, pious, pleasant, gentle, strong, patient, faithful, prudent, long-suffering, courageous, and never seeking its own; for wheresoever we seek our own, there we falleth from love.
-Thomas á Kempis

ENDNOTES TO SECTION 2

[1] 2 Corinthians 12:4
[2] Galatians 1:11-12
[3] Acts 20:9
[4] 1 Corinthians 13:1-8
[5] 1 Corinthians 13:11
[6] 1 Corinthians 13:13
[7] Hebrews 11:6
[8] Hebrews 6:19
[9] Matthew 22:36-38
[10] The English versions of the ancient Greek words are sometimes spelled differently by different translators.
[11] Isaiah 43:4, NIV, NASB
[12] John 21:15-17
[13] Luke 22:34
[14] John 21:18-19
[15] 1 Corinthians 3:1
[16] Hebrews 5:14
[17] Hebrews 6:1, NIV
[18] Hebrews 6:19-20a, NIV
[19] Hebrews 11:6, NIV
[20] Ephesians 2:8
[21] 1 Corinthians 13:2
[22] Matthew 10:8
[23] 2 Corinthians 12:4
[24] 2 Corinthians 12:7
[25] Matthew 15:18-19
[26] Matthew 22:37
[27] Matthew 22:39
[28] John 15:12
[29] 1 Corinthians 13:11
[30] 1 Corinthians 14:1
[31] 1 Corinthians 14:1 (Instead of "Pursue," which is also used by

the NASB, the KJV uses "Follow after, and the NIV uses "Follow the way of love.)

[32] Ephesians 2:18
[33] Matthew 22:40
[34] Galatians 5:14
[35] Philippians 2:13
[36] Philippians 2:12
[37] 1 John 4:8
[38] John 14:21
[39] 1 John 4:16, NIV
[40] John 3:30
[41] Philippians 2:3b, NIV
[42] 2 Corinthians 12:11
[43] Ephesians 3:8, NIV
[44] Philippians 4:11, NIV
[45] Hebrews 5:8
[46] Philippians 3:12-14
[47] Romans 5:5
[48] Philippians 2:13
[49] Romans 8:28
[50] James 1:17
[51] *In the Face of Surrender* by Richard Wurmbrand ©1998 (Bridge-Logos Publishers, North Brunswick, NJ)
[52] Genesis 13:8-9
[53] Genesis 13:10-11
[54] Genesis 14:14
[55] Genesis 14:23
[56] John 15:13
[57] *The New Foxes Book of Martyrs* by John Foxe ©1997 (Bridge-Logos Publishers, North Brunswick, NJ)

ADDENDUM

LOVE

AS LISTED IN NAVE'S TOPICAL BIBLE

(**Boldface** identifies some, but not all, of the passages or verses that speak of or demonstrate agape. All verses are from the King James Version of the Bible.)

(**Genesis 14:14-16**) **And when Abram heard that his brother was taken captive, he armed his trained servants, born in his own house, three hundred and eighteen, and pursued them unto Dan.**

And he divided himself against them, he and his servants, by night, and smote them, and pursued them unto Hobah, which is on the left hand of Damascus.

And he brought back all the goods, and also brought again his brother Lot, and his goods, and the women also, and the people.

(**Exodus 20:6**) **And showing mercy unto thousands of them that love me, and keep my commandments.**

(Exodus 32:31-32) And Moses returned unto the LORD, and said, Oh, this people have sinned a great sin, and have made them gods of gold.

Yet now, if thou wilt forgive their sin—; and if not, blot me, I pray thee, out of thy book which thou hast written.

(Leviticus 19:18) Thou shalt not avenge, nor bear any grudge against the children of thy people, but **thou shalt love thy neighbour as thyself**: I am the LORD.

(Leviticus 19:34) But the stranger that dwelleth with you shall be unto you as one born among you, and **thou shalt love him as thyself**; for ye were strangers in the land of Egypt: I am the LORD your God.

(Deuteronomy 5:10) And showing mercy unto thousands of them that love me and keep my commandments.

(Deuteronomy 6:5) And thou shalt love the LORD thy God with all thine heart, and with all thy soul, and with all thy might.

(Deuteronomy 7:9) Know therefore that the LORD thy God, he is God, the faithful God, which keepeth covenant and mercy with them that love him and keep his commandments to a thousand generations;

(Deuteronomy 10:12) And now, Israel, what doth the LORD thy God require of thee, but to fear the LORD thy God, to walk in all his ways, and to love him, and to serve the LORD thy God with all thy heart and with all thy soul,

(Deuteronomy 10:19) **Love ye therefore the stranger:** for ye were strangers in the land of Egypt.

(Deuteronomy 11:1) Therefore thou shalt love the LORD thy God, and keep his charge, and his statutes, and his judgments, and his commandments, alway.

(Deuteronomy 11:13) And it shall come to pass, if ye shall hearken diligently unto my commandments which I command you this day, to love the LORD your God, and to serve him with all your heart and with all your soul,

(Deuteronomy 11:22) For if ye shall diligently keep all these commandments which I command you, to do them, to love the LORD your God, to walk in all his ways, and to cleave unto him;

(Deuteronomy 13:3) Thou shalt not hearken unto the words of that prophet, or that dreamer of dreams: for the LORD your God proveth you, to know whether ye love the LORD your God with all your heart and with all your soul.

(Deuteronomy 30:6) And the LORD thy God will circumcise thine heart, and the heart of thy seed, to love the LORD thy God with all thine heart, and with all thy soul, that thou mayest live.

(Deuteronomy 30:16) In that I command thee this day to love the LORD thy God, to walk in his ways, and to keep his commandments and his statutes and his judgments, that thou mayest live and multiply: and the LORD thy God shall bless thee in the land whither thou goest to possess it.

(Deuteronomy 30:20) That thou mayest love the LORD thy God, and that thou mayest obey his voice, and that thou mayest cleave unto him: for he is thy life, and the length of thy days: that thou mayest dwell in the land which the LORD sware unto thy fathers, to Abraham, to Isaac, and to Jacob, to give them.

(Joshua 22:5) But take diligent heed to do the commandment and the law, which Moses the servant of the LORD charged you, to love the LORD your God, and to walk in all his ways, and to keep his commandments, and to cleave unto him, and to serve him with all your heart and with all your soul.

(Joshua 23:11) Take good heed therefore unto yourselves, that ye love the LORD your God.

(Ruth 1:1-22) Now it came to pass in the days when the judges ruled, that there was a famine in the land. And a certain man of Bethlehemjudah went to sojourn in the country of Moab, he, and his wife, and his two sons.
And the name of the man was Elimelech, and the name of his wife Naomi, and the name of his two sons Mahlon and Chilion, Ephrathites of Bethlehemjudah. And they came into the country of Moab, and continued there.
And Elimelech Naomi's husband died; and she was left, and her two sons.
And they took them wives of the women of Moab; the name of the one was Orpah, and the name of the other Ruth: and they dwelled there about ten years.
And Mahlon and Chilion died also both of them; and the woman was left of her two sons and her husband.
Then she arose with her daughters in law, that she might return

95

from the country of Moab: for she had heard in the country of Moab how that the Lord had visited his people in giving them bread.

Wherefore she went forth out of the place where she was, and her two daughters in law with her; and they went on the way to return unto the land of Judah.

And Naomi said unto her two daughters in law, Go, return each to her mother's house: the LORD deal kindly with you, as ye have dealt with the dead, and with me.

The LORD grant you that ye may find rest, each of you in the house of her husband. Then she kissed them; and they lifted up their voice, and wept.

And they said unto her, Surely we will return with thee unto thy people.

And Naomi said, Turn again, my daughters: why will ye go with me? are there yet any more sons in my womb, that they may be your husbands?

Turn again, my daughters, go your way; for I am too old to have an husband. If I should say, I have hope, if I should have an husband also to night, and should also bear sons;

Would ye tarry for them till they were grown? would ye stay for them from having husbands? nay, my daughters; for it grieveth me much for your sakes that the hand of the LORD is gone out against me.

And they lifted up their voice, and wept again: and Orpah kissed her mother in law; but Ruth clave unto her.

And she said, Behold, thy sister in law is gone back unto her people, and unto her gods: return thou after thy sister in law.

And Ruth said, Entreat me not to leave thee, or to return from following after thee: for whither thou goest, I will go; and where thou lodgest, I will lodge: thy people shall be my people, and thy God my God:

Where thou diest, will I die, and there will I be buried: the LORD do so to me, and more also, if ought but death part thee and me.

When she saw that she was stedfastly minded to go with her, then she left speaking unto her.

So they two went until they came to Bethlehem. And it came to pass, when they were come to Bethlehem, that all the city was moved about them, and they said, Is this Naomi?

And she said unto them, Call me not Naomi, call me Mara: for the Almighty hath dealt very bitterly with me.

I went out full, and the LORD hath brought me home again empty: why then call ye me Naomi, seeing the LORD hath testified against me, and the Almighty hath afflicted me?

So Naomi returned, and Ruth the Moabitess, her daughter in law, with her, which returned out of the country of Moab: and they came to Bethlehem in the beginning of barley harvest.

(Ruth 2:1-23) And Naomi had a kinsman of her husband's, a mighty man of wealth, of the family of Elimelech; and his name was Boaz.

And Ruth the Moabitess said unto Naomi, Let me now go to the field, and glean ears of corn after him in whose sight I shall find grace. And she said unto her, Go, my daughter.

And she went, and came, and gleaned in the field after the reapers: and her hap was to light on a part of the field belonging unto Boaz, who was of the kindred of Elimelech.

And, behold, Boaz came from Bethlehem, and said unto the reapers, The LORD be with you. And they answered him, The LORD bless thee.

Then said Boaz unto his servant that was set over the reapers, Whose damsel is this?

And the servant that was set over the reapers answered and said, It is the Moabitish damsel that came back with Naomi out of the country of Moab:

And she said, I pray you, let me glean and gather after the reapers among the sheaves: so she came, and hath continued even from the morning until now, that she tarried a little in the house.

Then said Boaz unto Ruth, Hearest thou not, my daughter? Go not to glean in another field, neither go from hence, but abide here fast by my maidens:

Let thine eyes be on the field that they do reap, and go thou after them: have I not charged the young men that they shall not touch thee? and when thou art athirst, go unto the vessels, and drink of that which the young men have drawn.

Then she fell on her face, and bowed herself to the ground, and said unto him, Why have I found grace in thine eyes, that thou shouldest take knowledge of me, seeing I am a stranger?

And Boaz answered and said unto her, It hath fully been showed me, all that thou hast done unto thy mother in law since the death of thine husband: and how thou hast left thy father and thy mother, and the land of thy nativity, and art come unto a people which thou knewest not heretofore.

The LORD recompense thy work, and a full reward be given thee of the LORD God of Israel, under whose wings thou art come to trust.

Then she said, Let me find favour in thy sight, my lord; for that thou hast comforted me, and for that thou hast spoken friendly unto thine handmaid, though I be not like unto one of thine handmaidens.

And Boaz said unto her, At mealtime come thou hither, and eat of the bread, and dip thy morsel in the vinegar. And she sat beside the reapers: and he reached her parched corn, and she did eat, and was sufficed, and left.

And when she was risen up to glean, Boaz commanded his young men, saying, Let her glean even among the sheaves, and reproach her not:

And let fall also some of the handfuls of purpose for her, and leave them, that she may glean them, and rebuke her not.

So she gleaned in the field until even, and beat out that she had gleaned: and it was about an ephah of barley.

And she took it up, and went into the city: and her mother in law saw what she had gleaned: and she brought forth, and gave to her that she had reserved after she was sufficed.

And her mother in law said unto her, Where hast thou gleaned to day? and where wroughtest thou? blessed be he that did take knowledge of thee. And she showed her mother in law with whom she had wrought, and said, The man's name with whom I wrought to day is Boaz.

And Naomi said unto her daughter in law, Blessed be he of the LORD, who hath not left off his kindness to the living and to the dead. And Naomi said unto her, The man is near of kin unto us, one of our next kinsmen.

And Ruth the Moabitess said, He said unto me also, Thou shalt keep fast by my young men, until they have ended all my harvest.

And Naomi said unto Ruth her daughter in law, It is good, my daughter, that thou go out with his maidens, that they meet thee not in any other field.

So she kept fast by the maidens of Boaz to glean unto the end of barley harvest and of wheat harvest; and dwelt with her mother in law.

(Ruth 3:1) Then Naomi her mother in law said unto her, My daughter, shall I not seek rest for thee, that it may be well with thee?

And now is not Boaz of our kindred, with whose maidens thou wast? Behold, he winnoweth barley to night in the threshingfloor.

Wash thy self therefore, and anoint thee, and put thy raiment upon thee, and get thee down to the floor: but make not thyself known unto the man, until he shall have done eating and drinking.

And it shall be, when he lieth down, that thou shalt mark the place where he shall lie, and thou shalt go in, and uncover his feet, and lay thee down; and he will tell thee what thou shalt do.

And she said unto her, All that thou sayest unto me I will do.

And she went down unto the floor, and did according to all that her mother in law bade her.

And when Boaz had eaten and drunk, and his heart was merry, he went to lie down at the end of the heap of corn: and she came softly, and uncovered his feet, and laid her down.

And it came to pass at midnight, that the man was afraid, and turned himself: and, behold, a woman lay at his feet.

And he said, Who art thou? And she answered, I am Ruth thine handmaid: spread therefore thy skirt over thine handmaid; for thou art a near kinsman.

And he said, Blessed be thou of the LORD, my daughter: for thou hast showed more kindness in the latter end than at the beginning, inasmuch as thou followedst not young men, whether poor or rich.

And now, my daughter, fear not; I will do to thee all that thou requirest: for all the city of my people doth know that thou art a virtuous woman.

And now it is true that I am thy near kinsman: howbeit there is a kinsman nearer than I.

Tarry this night, and it shall be in the morning, that if he will perform unto thee the part of a kinsman, well; let him do the kinsman's part: but if he will not do the part of a kinsman to thee, then will I do the part of a kinsman to thee, as the LORD liveth: lie down until the morning.

And she lay at his feet until the morning: and she rose up before one could know another. And he said, Let it not be known that a woman came into the floor.

Also he said, Bring the veil that thou hast upon thee, and hold it. And when she held it, he measured six measures of barley, and laid it on her: and she went into the city.

And when she came to her mother in law, she said, Who art thou, my daughter? And she told her all that the man had done to her.

And she said, These six measures of barley gave he me; for he said to me, Go not empty unto thy mother in law.

Then said she, Sit still, my daughter, until thou know how the matter will fall: for the man will not be in rest, until he have finished the thing this day.

(2 Samuel 15:30) And David went up by the ascent of mount Olivet, and wept as he went up, and had his head covered, and he went barefoot: and all the people that was with him covered every man his head, and they went up, weeping as they went up.

(2 Samuel 17:27-29) And it came to pass, when David was come to Mahanaim, that Shobi the son of Nahash of Rabbah of the children of Ammon, and Machir the son of Ammiel of Lodebar, and Barzillai the Gileadite of Rogelim,
Brought beds, and basins, and earthen vessels, and wheat, and barley, and flour, and parched corn, and beans, and lentiles, and parched pulse,
And honey, and butter, and sheep, and cheese of kine, for David, and for the people that were with him, to eat: for they said, The people is hungry, and weary, and thirsty, in the wilderness.

(1 Kings 18:4) For it was so, when Jezebel cut off the prophets of the LORD, that Obadiah took an hundred prophets, and hid them by fifty in a cave, and fed them with bread and water.)

(2 Chronicles 22:11) But Jehoshabeath, the daughter of the king, took Joash the son of Ahaziah, and stole him from among the king's sons that were slain, and put him and his nurse in a bedchamber. So Jehoshabeath, the daughter of king Jehoram, the wife of Jehoiada the priest, (for she was the sister of Ahaziah,) hid him from Athaliah, so that she slew him not.

(Nehemiah 5:10-15) I likewise, and my brethren, and my servants, might exact of them money and corn: I pray you, let us leave off this usury.
Restore, I pray you, to them, even this day, their lands, their vineyards, their oliveyards, and their houses, also the hundredth part of the money, and of the corn, the wine, and the oil, that ye exact of them.
Then said they, We will restore them, and will require nothing of them; so will we do as thou sayest. Then I called the priests, and took an oath of them, that they should do according to this promise.

Also I shook my lap, and said, So God shake out every man from his house, and from his labour, that performeth not this promise, even thus be he shaken out, and emptied. And all the congregation said, Amen, and praised the LORD. And the people did according to this promise.

Moreover from the time that I was appointed to be their governor in the land of Judah, from the twentieth year even unto the two and thirtieth year of Artaxerxes the king, that is, twelve years, I and my brethren have not eaten the bread of the governor.

But the former governors that had been before me were chargeable unto the people, and had taken of them bread and wine, beside forty shekels of silver; yea, even their servants bare rule over the people: but so did not I, because of the fear of God.

(Esther 2:7) And he brought up Hadassah, that is, Esther, his uncle's daughter: for she had neither father nor mother, and the maid was fair and beautiful; whom Mordecai, when her father and mother were dead, took for his own daughter.

(Job 42:11) Then came there unto him all his brethren, and all his sisters, and all they that had been of his acquaintance before, and did eat bread with him in his house: and they bemoaned him, and comforted him over all the evil that the LORD had brought upon him: every man also gave him a piece of money, and every one an earring of gold.

(Psalm 18:1) To the chief Musician, A Psalm of David, the servant of the LORD, who spake unto the LORD the words of this song in the day that the LORD delivered him from the hand of all his enemies, and from the hand of Saul: And he said, I will love thee, O LORD, my strength.

(Psalm 31:23) O love the LORD, all ye his saints: for the LORD preserveth the faithful, and plentifully rewardeth the proud doer.

(Psalm 37:4) Delight thyself also in the LORD; and he shall give thee the desires of thine heart.

(Psalm 45:10) Hearken, O daughter, and consider, and incline thine ear; forget also thine own people, and thy father's house;

(Psalm 45:11) So shall the king greatly desire thy beauty: for he is thy Lord; and worship thou him.

(Psalm 63:5) My soul shall be satisfied as with marrow and fatness; and my mouth shall praise thee with joyful lips:

(Psalm 63:6) When I remember thee upon my bed, and meditate on thee in the night watches.

(Psalm 69:35) For God will save Zion, and will build the cities of Judah: that they may dwell there, and have it in possession.

(Psalm 69:36) The seed also of his servants shall inherit it: and they that love his name shall dwell therein.

(Psalm 73:25) Whom have I in heaven but thee? and there is none upon earth that I desire beside thee.

(Psalm 73:26) My flesh and my heart faileth: but God is the strength of my heart, and my portion for ever.

(Psalm 91:14) Because he hath set his love upon me, therefore will I deliver him: I will set him on high, because he hath known my name.

(Psalm 97:10) Ye that love the LORD, hate evil: he preserveth the souls of his saints; he delivereth them out of the hand of the wicked.

(Psalm 116:1) I love the LORD, because he hath heard my voice and my supplications.

(Psalm 133:1-3) A Song of degrees of David. Behold, how good and how pleasant it is for brethren to dwell together in unity!
It is like the precious ointment upon the head, that ran down upon the beard, even Aaron's beard: that went down to the skirts of his garments;
As the dew of Hermon, and as the dew that descended upon the mountains of Zion: for there the LORD commanded the blessing, even life for evermore.

(Psalm 145:20) The LORD preserveth all them that love him: but all the wicked will he destroy.

(Proverb 8:17) I love them that love me; and those that seek me early shall find me.

(Proverb 10:12) Hatred stirreth up strifes: **but love covereth all sins.**

(Proverb 15:17) Better is a dinner of herbs where love is, than a stalled ox and hatred therewith.

(Proverb 17:9) He that covereth a transgression seeketh love; but he that repeateth a matter separateth very friends.

(Proverb 17:17) **A friend loveth at all times,** and a brother is born for adversity.

(Proverb 23:26) My son, give me thine heart, and let thine eyes observe my ways.

(Proverb 24:17-18) Rejoice not when thine enemy falleth, and let not thine heart be glad when he stumbleth:
Lest the LORD see it, and it displease him, and he turn away his wrath from him.

(Song 8:6) Set me as a seal upon thine heart, as a seal upon thine arm: for love is strong as death; jealousy is cruel as the grave: the coals thereof are coals of fire, which hath a most vehement flame.

(Song 8:7) **Many waters cannot quench love, neither can the floods drown it:** if a man would give all the substance of his house for love, it would utterly be contemned.

(Isaiah 56:6-7) Also the sons of the stranger, that join themselves to the LORD, to serve him, and to love the name of the LORD, to be his servants, every one that keepeth the sabbath from polluting it, and taketh hold of my covenant;
Even them will I bring to my holy mountain, and make them joyful in my house of prayer: their burnt offerings and their sacrifices shall be accepted upon mine altar; for mine house shall be called an house of prayer for all people.

(Jeremiah 2:2) Go and cry in the ears of Jerusalem, saying, Thus saith the LORD; I remember thee, the kindness of thy youth, the love of thine espousals, when thou wentest after me in the wilderness, in a land that was not sown.

(Jeremiah 2:3) Israel was holiness unto the LORD, and the firstfruits of his increase: all that devour him shall offend; evil shall come upon them, saith the LORD.

(Matthew 5:41-47) And whosoever shall compel thee to go a mile, go with him twain.

Give to him that asketh thee, and from him that would borrow of thee turn not thou away.

Ye have heard that it hath been said, Thou shalt love thy neighbour, and hate thine enemy.

But I say unto you, Love your enemies, bless them that curse you, do good to them that hate you, and pray for them which despitefully use you, and persecute you;

That ye may be the children of your Father which is in heaven: for he maketh his sun to rise on the evil and on the good, and sendeth rain on the just and on the unjust.

For if ye love them which love you, what reward have ye? do not even the publicans the same?

And if ye salute your brethren only, what do ye more than others? do not even the publicans so?

(Matthew 7:12) Therefore all things whatsoever ye would that men should do to you, do ye even so to them: for this is the law and the prophets.

(Matthew 10:37) He that loveth father or mother more than me is not worthy of me: and he that loveth son or daughter more than me is not worthy of me.

(Matthew 10:38) And he that taketh not his cross, and followeth after me, is not worthy of me.

(Matthew 10:41) He that receiveth a prophet in the name of a prophet shall receive a prophet's reward; and he that receiveth a righteous man in the name of a righteous man shall receive a righteous man's reward.

(Matthew 10:42) And whosoever shall give to drink unto one of these little ones a cup of cold water only in the name of a disciple, verily I say unto you, he shall in no wise lose his reward.

(Matthew 17:4) Then answered Peter, and said unto Jesus, Lord, it is good for us to be here: if thou wilt, let us make here three tabernacles; one for thee, and one for Moses, and one for Elias.

(Matthew 19:19) Honour thy father and thy mother: and, Thou shalt love thy neighbour as thyself.

(Matthew 22:37-38) Jesus said unto him, Thou shalt love the Lord thy God with all thy heart, and with all thy soul, and with all thy mind.
This is the first and great commandment.

(Matthew 25:34-40) Then shall the King say unto them on his right hand, Come, ye blessed of my Father, inherit the kingdom prepared for you from the foundation of the world:
For I was an hungered, and ye gave me meat: I was thirsty, and ye gave me drink: I was a stranger, and ye took me in:
Naked, and ye clothed me: I was sick, and ye visited me: I was in prison, and ye came unto me.
Then shall the righteous answer him, saying, Lord, when saw we thee an hungered, and fed thee? or thirsty, and gave thee drink?
When saw we thee a stranger, and took thee in? or naked, and clothed thee?
Or when saw we thee sick, or in prison, and came unto thee?
And the King shall answer and say unto them, Verily I say unto you, Inasmuch as ye have done it unto one of the least of these my brethren, ye have done it unto me.

(Matthew 26:6-13) Now when Jesus was in Bethany, in the house of Simon the leper,
There came unto him a woman having an alabaster box of very precious ointment, and poured it on his head, as he sat at meat.
But when his disciples saw it, they had indignation, saying, To what purpose is this waste?
For this ointment might have been sold for much, and given to the poor.
When Jesus understood it, he said unto them, Why trouble ye the woman? for she hath wrought a good work upon me.
For ye have the poor always with you; but me ye have not always.

For in that she hath poured this ointment on my body, she did it for my burial.

Verily I say unto you, Wheresoever this gospel shall be preached in the whole world, there shall also this, that this woman hath done, be told for a memorial of her.

(Matthew 27:55-61) And many women were there beholding afar off, which followed Jesus from Galilee, ministering unto him:

Among which was Mary Magdalene, and Mary the mother of James and Joses, and the mother of Zebedee's children.

When the even was come, there came a rich man of Arimathaea, named Joseph, who also himself was Jesus' disciple:

He went to Pilate, and begged the body of Jesus. Then Pilate commanded the body to be delivered.

And when Joseph had taken the body, he wrapped it in a clean linen cloth,

And laid it in his own new tomb, which he had hewn out in the rock: and he rolled a great stone to the door of the sepulchre, and departed.

And there was Mary Magdalene, and the other Mary, sitting over against the sepulchre.

(Matthew 28:1-9) In the end of the sabbath, as it began to dawn toward the first day of the week, came Mary Magdalene and the other Mary to see the sepulchre.

And, behold, there was a great earthquake: for the angel of the Lord descended from heaven, and came and rolled back the stone from the door, and sat upon it.

His countenance was like lightning, and his raiment white as snow:

And for fear of him the keepers did shake, and became as dead men.

And the angel answered and said unto the women, Fear not ye: for I know that ye seek Jesus, which was crucified.

He is not here: for he is risen, as he said. Come, see the place where the Lord lay.

And go quickly, and tell his disciples that he is risen from the dead; and, behold, he goeth before you into Galilee; there shall ye see him: lo, I have told you.

And they departed quickly from the sepulchre with fear and great joy; and did run to bring his disciples word.

And as they went to tell his disciples, behold, Jesus met them, saying, All hail. And they came and held him by the feet, and worshipped him.

(Mark 5:18) And when he was come into the ship, he that had been possessed with the devil prayed him that he might be with him.

(Mark 9:41) For whosoever shall give you a cup of water to drink in my name, because ye belong to Christ, verily I say unto you, he shall not lose his reward.

(Mark 12:29-33) And Jesus answered him, The first of all the commandments is, Hear, O Israel; The Lord our God is one Lord:

And thou shalt love the Lord thy God with all thy heart, and with all thy soul, and with all thy mind, and with all thy strength: this is the first commandment.

And the second is like, namely this, Thou shalt love thy neighbour as thyself. There is none other commandment greater than these.

And the scribe said unto him, Well, Master, thou hast said the truth: for there is one God; and there is none other but he:

And to love him with all the heart, and with all the understanding, and with all the soul, and with all the strength, and to love his neighbour as himself, is more than all whole burnt offerings and sacrifices.

(Mark 16:10) And she went and told them that had been with him, as they mourned and wept.

(Luke 2:29-30) Lord, now lettest thou thy servant depart in peace, according to thy word:
For mine eyes have seen thy salvation,

(Luke 6:31) And as ye would that men should do to you, do ye also to them likewise.

(Luke 6:32-35) For if ye love them which love you, what thank have ye? for sinners also love those that love them.

And if ye do good to them which do good to you, what thank have ye? for sinners also do even the same.

And if ye lend to them of whom ye hope to receive, what

thank have ye? for sinners also lend to sinners, to receive as much again.

But love ye your enemies, and do good, and lend, hoping for nothing again; and your reward shall be great, and ye shall be the children of the Highest: for he is kind unto the unthankful and to the evil.

(Luke 7:2-6) And a certain centurion's servant, who was dear unto him, was sick, and ready to die.

And when he heard of Jesus, he sent unto him the elders of the Jews, beseeching him that he would come and heal his servant.

And when they came to Jesus, they besought him instantly, saying, That he was worthy for whom he should do this:

For he loveth our nation, and he hath built us a synagogue.

Then Jesus went with them. And when he was now not far from the house, the centurion sent friends to him, saying unto him, **Lord, trouble not thyself: for I am not worthy that thou shouldest enter under my roof:**

(Luke 7:47) Wherefore I say unto thee, Her sins, which are many, are forgiven; for she loved much: but to whom little is forgiven, the same loveth little.

(Luke 8:2-3) And certain women, which had been healed of evil spirits and infirmities, Mary called Magdalene, out of whom went seven devils,

And Joanna the wife of Chuza Herod's steward, and Susanna, and many others, which ministered unto him of their substance.

(Luke 10:25-37) And, behold, a certain lawyer stood up, and tempted him, saying, Master, what shall I do to inherit eternal life?

He said unto him, What is written in the law? how readest thou?

And he answering said, Thou shalt love the Lord thy God with all thy heart, and with all thy soul, and with all thy strength, and with all thy mind; and thy neighbour as thyself.

And he said unto him, Thou hast answered right: this do, and thou shalt live.

But he, willing to justify himself, said unto Jesus, And who is my neighbour?

And Jesus answering said, A certain man went down from Jerusalem to Jericho, and fell among thieves, which stripped him of his raiment, and wounded him, and departed, leaving him half dead.

And by chance there came down a certain priest that way: and when he saw him, he passed by on the other side.

And likewise a Levite, when he was at the place, came and looked on him, and passed by on the other side.

But a certain Samaritan, as he journeyed, came where he was: and when he saw him, he had compassion on him,

And went to him, and bound up his wounds, pouring in oil and wine, and set him on his own beast, and brought him to an inn, and took care of him.

And on the morrow when he departed, he took out two pence, and gave them to the host, and said unto him, Take care of him; and whatsoever thou spendest more, when I come again, I will repay thee.

Which now of these three, thinkest thou, was neighbour unto him that fell among the thieves?

And he said, He that showed mercy on him. Then said Jesus unto him, Go, and do thou likewise.

(Luke 10:39) And she had a sister called Mary, which also sat at Jesus' feet, and heard his word.

(Luke 11:42) But woe unto you, Pharisees! for ye tithe mint and rue and all manner of herbs, and pass over judgment and the love of God: these ought ye to have done, and not to leave the other undone.

(Luke 23:27) And there followed him a great company of people, and of women, which also bewailed and lamented him.

(Luke 23:55-24:10) And the women also, which came with him from Galilee, followed after, and beheld the sepulchre, and how his body was laid.

And they returned, and prepared spices and ointments; and rested the sabbath day according to the commandment.

Now upon the first day of the week, very early in the morning, they came unto the sepulchre, bringing the spices which they had prepared, and certain others with them.

And they found the stone rolled away from the sepulchre.

And they entered in, and found not the body of the Lord Jesus.

And it came to pass, as they were much perplexed thereabout, behold, two men stood by them in shining garments:

And as they were afraid, and bowed down their faces to the earth, they said unto them, Why seek ye the living among the dead?

He is not here, but is risen: remember how he spake unto you when he was yet in Galilee,

Saying, The Son of man must be delivered into the hands of sinful men, and be crucified, and the third day rise again.

And they remembered his words,

And returned from the sepulchre, and told all these things unto the eleven, and to all the rest.

It was Mary Magdalene, and Joanna, and Mary the mother of James, and other women that were with them, which told these things unto the apostles.

(Luke 24:17-41) And he said unto them, What manner of communications are these that ye have one to another, as ye walk, and are sad?

And the one of them, whose name was Cleopas, answering said unto him, Art thou only a stranger in Jerusalem, and hast not known the things which are come to pass there in these days?

And he said unto them, What things? And they said unto him, Concerning Jesus of Nazareth, which was a prophet mighty in deed and word before God and all the people:

And how the chief priests and our rulers delivered him to be condemned to death, and have crucified him.

But we trusted that it had been he which should have redeemed Israel: and beside all this, to day is the third day since these things were done.

Yea, and certain women also of our company made us astonished, which were early at the sepulchre;

And when they found not his body, they came, saying, that they had also seen a vision of angels, which said that he was alive.

And certain of them which were with us went to the sepulchre, and found it even so as the women had said: but him they saw not.

Then he said unto them, O fools, and slow of heart to believe all that the prophets have spoken:

Ought not Christ to have suffered these things, and to enter into his glory?

And beginning at Moses and all the prophets, he expounded unto them in all the scriptures the things concerning himself.

And they drew nigh unto the village, whither they went: and he made as though he would have gone further.

But they constrained him, saying, Abide with us: for it is toward evening, and the day is far spent. And he went in to tarry with them.

And it came to pass, as he sat at meat with them, he took bread, and blessed it, and brake, and gave to them.

And their eyes were opened, and they knew him; and he vanished out of their sight.

And they said one to another, Did not our heart burn within us, while he talked with us by the way, and while he opened to us the scriptures?

And they rose up the same hour, and returned to Jerusalem, and found the eleven gathered together, and them that were with them,

Saying, The Lord is risen indeed, and hath appeared to Simon.

And they told what things were done in the way, and how he was known of them in breaking of bread.

And as they thus spake, Jesus himself stood in the midst of them, and saith unto them, Peace be unto you.

But they were terrified and affrighted, and supposed that they had seen a spirit.

And he said unto them, Why are ye troubled? and why do thoughts arise in your hearts?

Behold my hands and my feet, that it is I myself: handle me, and see; for a spirit hath not flesh and bones, as ye see me have.

And when he had thus spoken, he showed them his hands and his feet.

And while they yet believed not for joy, and wondered, he said unto them, Have ye here any meat?

(John 5:42) But I know you, that ye have not the love of God in you.

(John 8:42) Jesus said unto them, If God were your Father, ye would love me: for I proceeded forth and came from God; neither came I of myself, but he sent me.

(John 11:16) Then said Thomas, which is called Didymus, unto his fellowdisciples, Let us also go, that we may die with him.

(John 12:3-8) Then took Mary a pound of ointment of spikenard, very costly, and anointed the feet of Jesus, and wiped his feet with her hair: and the house was filled with the odour of the ointment.

Then saith one of his disciples, Judas Iscariot, Simon's son, which should betray him,

Why was not this ointment sold for three hundred pence, and given to the poor?

This he said, not that he cared for the poor; but because he was a thief, and had the bag, and bare what was put therein.

Then said Jesus, Let her alone: against the day of my burying hath she kept this.

For the poor always ye have with you; but me ye have not always.

(John 13:14) If I then, your Lord and Master, have washed your feet; ye also ought to wash one another's feet.

For I have given you an example, that ye should do as I have done to you.

(John 13:34-35) A new commandment I give unto you, That ye love one another; as I have loved you, that ye also love one another.

By this shall all men know that ye are my disciples, if ye have love one to another.

(John 13:37) Peter said unto him, Lord, why cannot I follow thee now? I will lay down my life for thy sake.

(John 14:15) If ye love me, keep my commandments.

(John 14:21) **He that hath my commandments, and keepeth them, he it is that loveth me:** and he that loveth me shall be loved of my Father, and I will love him, and will manifest myself to him.

(John 14:23) Jesus answered and said unto him, **If a man love me, he will keep my words:** and my Father will love him, and we will come unto him, and make our abode with him.

(John 14:28) Ye have heard how I said unto you, I go away, and come again unto you. If ye loved me, ye would rejoice, because I said, I go unto the Father: for my Father is greater than I.

(John 15:9) As the Father hath loved me, so have I loved you: continue ye in my love.

(John 15:12-13) This is my commandment, That ye love one another, as I have loved you.
Greater love hath no man than this, that a man lay down his life for his friends.

(John 15:17) These things I command you, that ye love one another.

(John 16:27) For the Father himself loveth you, because ye have loved me, and have believed that I came out from God.

(John 17:26) And I have declared unto them thy name, and will declare it: that the love wherewith thou hast loved me may be in them, and I in them.

(John 18:10) Then Simon Peter having a sword drew it, and smote the high priest's servant, and cut off his right ear. The servant's name was Malchus.

(John 19:39-40) And there came also Nicodemus, which at the first came to Jesus by night, and brought a mixture of myrrh and aloes, about an hundred pound weight.
Then took they the body of Jesus, and wound it in linen clothes with the spices, as the manner of the Jews is to bury.

(John 20:1-6) The first day of the week cometh Mary Magdalene early, when it was yet dark, unto the sepulchre, and seeth the stone taken away from the sepulchre.
Then she runneth, and cometh to Simon Peter, and to the other disciple, whom Jesus loved, and saith unto them, They have taken away the Lord out of the sepulchre, and we know not where they have laid him.
Peter therefore went forth, and that other disciple, and came to the sepulchre.
So they ran both together: and the other disciple did outrun Peter, and came first to the sepulchre.
And he stooping down, and looking in, saw the linen clothes lying; yet went he not in.
Then cometh Simon Peter following him, and went into the sepulchre, and seeth the linen clothes lie,

(John 20:11-18) But Mary stood without at the sepulchre weeping: and as she wept, she stooped down, and looked into the sepulchre,

And seeth two angels in white sitting, the one at the head, and the other at the feet, where the body of Jesus had lain.

And they say unto her, Woman, why weepest thou? She saith unto them, Because they have taken away my Lord, and I know not where they have laid him.

And when she had thus said, she turned herself back, and saw Jesus standing, and knew not that it was Jesus.

Jesus saith unto her, Woman, why weepest thou? whom seekest thou? She, supposing him to be the gardener, saith unto him, Sir, if thou have borne him hence, tell me where thou hast laid him, and I will take him away.

Jesus saith unto her, Mary. She turned herself, and saith unto him, Rabboni; which is to say, Master.

Jesus saith unto her, Touch me not; for I am not yet ascended to my Father: but go to my brethren, and say unto them, I ascend unto my Father, and your Father; and to my God, and your God.

Mary Magdalene came and told the disciples that she had seen the Lord, and that he had spoken these things unto her.

(John 20:20) And when he had so said, he showed unto them his hands and his side. Then were the disciples glad, when they saw the Lord.

(John 21:7) Therefore that disciple whom Jesus loved saith unto Peter, It is the Lord. Now when Simon Peter heard that it was the Lord, he girt his fisher's coat unto him, (for he was naked,) and did cast himself into the sea.

(John 21:17) He saith unto him the third time, **Simon, son of Jonas, lovest thou me?** Peter was grieved because he said unto him the third time, Lovest thou me? And he said unto him, Lord, thou knowest all things; thou knowest that I love thee. Jesus saith unto him, Feed my sheep.

(Acts 20:26-17) Wherefore I take you to record this day, that I am pure from the blood of all men.

For I have not shunned to declare unto you all the counsel of God.

114

(Acts 20:31) Therefore watch, and remember, that by the space of three years I ceased not to warn every one night and day with tears.

(Acts 21:13) Then Paul answered, What mean ye to weep and to break mine heart? for **I am ready not to be bound only, but also to die at Jerusalem for the name of the Lord Jesus.**

(Acts 26:29) And Paul said, I would to God, that not only thou, but also all that hear me this day, were both almost, and altogether such as I am, except these bonds.

(Acts 28:15) And from thence, when the brethren heard of us, they came to meet us as far as Appii forum, and The three taverns: whom when Paul saw, he thanked God, and took courage.

(Romans 1:12) That is, that I may be comforted together with you by the mutual faith both of you and me.

(Romans 5:5) And hope maketh not ashamed; because **the love of God is shed abroad in our hearts by the Holy Ghost which is given unto us.**

(Romans 5:7) For scarcely for a righteous man will one die: yet peradventure for a good man some would even dare to die.

(Romans 8:28) And we know that all things work together for good to them that love God, to them who are the called according to his purpose.

(Romans 9:1) I say the truth in Christ, I lie not, my conscience also bearing me witness in the Holy Ghost,

(Romans 9:2-3) That I have great heaviness and continual sorrow in my heart.
For I could wish that myself were accursed from Christ for my brethren, my kinsmen according to the flesh:

(Romans 12:9-10) Let love be without dissimulation. Abhor that which is evil; cleave to that which is good.
Be kindly affectioned one to another with brotherly love; in honour preferring one another;

115

(Romans 12:15-16) Rejoice with them that do rejoice, and weep with them that weep.

Be of the same mind one toward another. Mind not high things, but condescend to men of low estate. Be not wise in your own conceits.

(Romans 13:8-10) Owe no man any thing, but to love one another: for he that loveth another hath fulfilled the law.

For this, Thou shalt not commit adultery, Thou shalt not kill, Thou shalt not steal, Thou shalt not bear false witness, Thou shalt not covet; and if there be any other commandment, it is briefly comprehended in this saying, namely, Thou shalt love thy neighbour as thyself.

Love worketh no ill to his neighbour: therefore love is the fulfilling of the law.

(Romans 14:19) Let us therefore follow after the things which make for peace, and things wherewith one may edify another.

(Romans 14:21) It is good neither to eat flesh, nor to drink wine, nor any thing whereby thy brother stumbleth, or is offended, or is made weak.

(Romans 15:1-2) We then that are strong ought to bear the infirmities of the weak, and not to please ourselves.

Let every one of us please his neighbour for his good to edification.

(Romans 15:5) Now the God of patience and consolation grant you to be likeminded one toward another according to Christ Jesus:

(Romans 15:7) Wherefore receive ye one another, as Christ also received us to the glory of God.

(Romans 15:14-15) And I myself also am persuaded of you, my brethren, that ye also are full of goodness, filled with all knowledge, able also to admonish one another.

Nevertheless, brethren, I have written the more boldly unto you in some sort, as putting you in mind, because of the grace that is given to me of God,

(Romans 15:24) Whensoever I take my journey into Spain, I will come to you: for I trust to see you in my journey, and to be brought on my way thitherward by you, if first I be somewhat filled with your company.

(Romans 15:32) That I may come unto you with joy by the will of God, and may with you be refreshed.

(Romans 16:1-16) I commend unto you Phebe our sister, which is a servant of the church which is at Cenchrea:
That ye receive her in the Lord, as becometh saints, and that ye assist her in whatsoever business she hath need of you: **for she hath been a succourer of many, and of myself also.**
Greet Priscilla and Aquila my helpers in Christ Jesus:
Who have for my life laid down their own necks: unto whom not only I give thanks, but also all the churches of the Gentiles.
Likewise greet the church that is in their house. Salute my well beloved Epaenetus, who is the firstfruits of Achaia unto Christ.
Greet Mary, who bestowed much labour on us.
Salute Andronicus and Junia, my kinsmen, and my fellow prisoners, who are of note among the apostles, who also were in Christ before me.
Greet Amplias my beloved in the Lord.
Salute Urbane, our helper in Christ, and Stachys my beloved.
Salute Apelles approved in Christ. Salute them which are of Aristobulus' household.
Salute Herodion my kinsman. Greet them that be of the household of Narcissus, which are in the Lord.
Salute Tryphena and Tryphosa, who labour in the Lord. Salute the beloved Persis, which laboured much in the Lord.
Salute Rufus chosen in the Lord, and his mother and mine.
Salute Asyncritus, Phlegon, Hermas, Patrobas, Hermes, and the brethren which are with them.
Salute Philologus, and Julia, Nereus, and his sister, and Olympas, and all the saints which are with them.
Salute one another with an holy kiss. The churches of Christ salute you.

(Romans 16:19) For your obedience is come abroad unto all men. I am glad therefore on your behalf: but yet I would have you wise unto that which is good, and simple concerning evil.

(1 Corinthians 1:4) I thank my God always on your behalf, for the grace of God which is given you by Jesus Christ;

(1 Corinthians 4:14-16) I write not these things to shame you, but as my beloved sons I warn you.

For though ye have ten thousand instructors in Christ, yet have ye not many fathers: for in Christ Jesus I have begotten you through the gospel.

Wherefore I beseech you, be ye followers of me.

(1 Corinthians 8:1) Now as touching things offered unto idols, we know that we all have knowledge. Knowledge puffeth up, but **charity edifieth.**

(1 Corinthians 8:3) But if any man love God, the same is known of him.

(1 Corinthians 8:13) Wherefore, if meat make my brother to offend, I will eat no flesh while the world standeth, lest I make my brother to offend.

(1 Corinthians 10:24) Let no man seek his own, but every man another's wealth.

(1 Corinthians 13:1-13) Though I speak with the tongues of men and of angels, and have not charity, I am become as sounding brass, or a tinkling cymbal.

And though I have the gift of prophecy, and understand all mysteries, and all knowledge; and though I have all faith, so that I could remove mountains, and have not charity, I am nothing.

And though I bestow all my goods to feed the poor, and though I give my body to be burned, and have not charity, it profiteth me nothing.

Charity suffereth long, and is kind; charity envieth not; charity vaunteth not itself, is not puffed up,

Doth not behave itself unseemly, seeketh not her own, is not easily provoked, thinketh no evil;

Rejoiceth not in iniquity, but rejoiceth in the truth;

Beareth all things, believeth all things, hopeth all things, endureth all things.

Charity never faileth: but whether there be prophecies, they shall fail; whether there be tongues, they shall cease; whether there

be knowledge, it shall vanish away.

For we know in part, and we prophesy in part.

But when that which is perfect is come, then that which is in part shall be done away.

When I was a child, I spake as a child, I understood as a child, I thought as a child: but when I became a man, I put away childish things.

For now we see through a glass, darkly; but then face to face: now I know in part; but then shall I know even as also I am known.

And now abideth faith, hope, charity, these three; but the greatest of these is charity.

(1 Corinthians 14:1) Follow after charity, and desire spiritual gifts, but rather that ye may prophesy.

(1 Corinthians 16:14) Let all your things be done with charity.

(1 Corinthians 16:22) If any man love not the Lord Jesus Christ, let him be Anathema Maranatha.

(2 Corinthians 1:3-6) Blessed be God, even the Father of our Lord Jesus Christ, the Father of mercies, and the God of all comfort;

Who comforteth us in all our tribulation, that we may be able to comfort them which are in any trouble, by the comfort wherewith we ourselves are comforted of God.

For as the sufferings of Christ abound in us, so our consolation also aboundeth by Christ.

And whether we be afflicted, it is for your consolation and salvation, which is effectual in the enduring of the same sufferings which we also suffer: or whether we be comforted, it is for your consolation and salvation.

(2 Corinthians 1:14) As also ye have acknowledged us in part, that we are your rejoicing, even as ye also are ours in the day of the Lord Jesus.

(2 Corinthians 1:23) Moreover I call God for a record upon my soul, that to spare you I came not as yet unto Corinth.

(2 Corinthians 1:24) Not for that we have dominion over your faith, but are helpers of your joy: for by faith ye stand.

(2 Corinthians 2:1-17) But I determined this with myself, that I would not come again to you in heaviness.

For if I make you sorry, who is he then that maketh me glad, but the same which is made sorry by me?

And I wrote this same unto you, lest, when I came, I should have sorrow from them of whom I ought to rejoice; having confidence in you all, that my joy is the joy of you all.

For out of much affliction and anguish of heart I wrote unto you with many tears; not that ye should be grieved, but that ye might know the love which I have more abundantly unto you.

But if any have caused grief, he hath not grieved me, but in part: that I may not overcharge you all.

Sufficient to such a man is this punishment, which was inflicted of many.

So that contrariwise ye ought rather to forgive him, and comfort him, lest perhaps such a one should be swallowed up with overmuch sorrow.

Wherefore I beseech you that ye would confirm your love toward him.

For to this end also did I write, that I might know the proof of you, whether ye be obedient in all things.

To whom ye forgive any thing, I forgive also: for if I forgave any thing, to whom I forgave it, for your sakes forgave I it in the person of Christ;

Lest Satan should get an advantage of us: for we are not ignorant of his devices.

Furthermore, when I came to Troas to preach Christ's gospel, and a door was opened unto me of the Lord,

I had no rest in my spirit, because I found not Titus my brother: but taking my leave of them, I went from thence into Macedonia.

Now thanks be unto God, which always causeth us to triumph in Christ, and maketh manifest the savour of his knowledge by us in every place.

For we are unto God a sweet savour of Christ, in them that are saved, and in them that perish:

To the one we are the savour of death unto death; and to the other the savour of life unto life. And who is sufficient for these things?

For we are not as many, which corrupt the word of God: but as of sincerity, but as of God, in the sight of God speak we in Christ.

(2 Corinthians 3:2) Ye are our epistle written in our hearts, known and read of all men:

(2 Corinthians 4:5) For we preach not ourselves, but Christ Jesus the Lord; and ourselves your servants for Jesus' sake.

(2 Corinthians 5:6) Therefore we are always confident, knowing that, whilst we are at home in the body, we are absent from the Lord:

(2 Corinthians 5:8) We are confident, I say, and willing rather to be absent from the body, and to be present with the Lord.

(2 Corinthians 5:14-15) **For the love of Christ constraineth us;** because we thus judge, that if one died for all, then were all dead:
And that he died for all, that they which live should not henceforth live unto themselves, but unto him which died for them, and rose again.

(2 Corinthians 6:4-7) But in all things approving ourselves as the ministers of God, in much patience, in afflictions, in necessities, in distresses,
In stripes, in imprisonments, in tumults, in labours, in watchings, in fastings;
By pureness, by knowledge, by longsuffering, by kindness, by the Holy Ghost, by love unfeigned,

(2 Corinthians 6:11-13) O ye Corinthians, our mouth is open unto you, our heart is enlarged.
Ye are not straitened in us, but ye are straitened in your own bowels.
Now for a recompense in the same, (I speak as unto my children,) be ye also enlarged.

(2 Corinthians 7:1-4) Having therefore these promises, dearly beloved, let us cleanse ourselves from all filthiness of the flesh and spirit, perfecting holiness in the fear of God.
Receive us; **we have wronged no man, we have corrupted no man, we have defrauded no man.**
I speak not this to condemn you: for I have said before, that ye are in our hearts to die and live with you.
Great is my boldness of speech toward you, great is my glorying

121

of you: I am filled with comfort, I am exceeding joyful in all our tribulation.

(2 Corinthians 7:7) And not by his coming only, but by the consolation wherewith he was comforted in you, when he told us your earnest desire, your mourning, your fervent mind toward me; so that I rejoiced the more.

(2 Corinthians 7:12) Wherefore, though I wrote unto you, I did it not for his cause that had done the wrong, nor for his cause that suffered wrong, but that our care for you in the sight of God might appear unto you.

(2 Corinthians 8:7-8) Therefore, as ye abound in every thing, in faith, and utterance, and knowledge, and in all diligence, and in your love to us, see that ye abound in this grace also.
I speak not by commandment, but by occasion of the forwardness of others, and **to prove the sincerity of your love.**

(2 Corinthians 11:2) For I am jealous over you with godly jealousy: for I have espoused you to one husband, that I may present you as a chaste virgin to Christ.

(2 Corinthians 12:14) Behold, the third time I am ready to come to you; and I will not be burdensome to you: for I seek not yours, but you: for the children ought not to lay up for the parents, but the parents for the children.
(2 Corinthians 12:15) And I will very gladly spend and be spent for you; though the more abundantly I love you, the less I be loved.
(2 Corinthians 12:16) But be it so, I did not burden you: nevertheless, being crafty, I caught you with guile.

(2 Corinthians 12:19-21) Again, think ye that we excuse ourselves unto you? we speak before God in Christ: but **we do all things, dearly beloved, for your edifying.**
For I fear, lest, when I come, I shall not find you such as I would, and that I shall be found unto you such as ye would not: lest there be debates, envyings, wraths, strifes, backbitings, whisperings, swellings, tumults:
And lest, when I come again, my God will humble me among you, and that I shall bewail many which have sinned already, and

have not repented of the uncleanness and fornication and lasciviousness which they have committed.

(2 Corinthians 13:9) For we are glad, when we are weak, and ye are strong: and this also we wish, even your perfection.

(Galatians 4:11) I am afraid of you, lest I have bestowed upon you labour in vain.

(Galatians 4:12-20) Brethren, I beseech you, be as I am; for I am as ye are: **ye have not injured me at all.**
Ye know how through infirmity of the flesh I preached the gospel unto you at the first.
And my temptation which was in my flesh ye despised not, nor rejected; but received me as an angel of God, even as Christ Jesus.
Where is then the blessedness ye spake of? for **I bear you record, that, if it had been possible, ye would have plucked out your own eyes, and have given them to me.**
Am I therefore become your enemy, because I tell you the truth?
They zealously affect you, but not well; yea, they would exclude you, that ye might affect them.
But it is good to be zealously affected always in a good thing, and not only when I am present with you.
My little children, of whom I travail in birth again until Christ be formed in you,
I desire to be present with you now, and to change my voice; for I stand in doubt of you.

(Galatians 5:6) For in Jesus Christ neither circumcision availeth any thing, nor uncircumcision; but **faith which worketh by love.**

(Galatians 5:13-14) For, brethren, ye have been called unto liberty; only use not liberty for an occasion to the flesh, but **by love serve one another.**
For all the law is fulfilled in one word, even in this; Thou shalt love thy neighbour as thyself.

(Galatians 5:22) But the fruit of the Spirit is love, joy, peace, longsuffering, gentleness, goodness, faith,

(Galatians 5:26) Let us not be desirous of vain glory, provoking one another, envying one another.

(Galatians 6:1-2) **Brethren, if a man be overtaken in a fault, ye which are spiritual, restore such an one in the spirit of meekness;** considering thyself, lest thou also be tempted.
Bear ye one another's burdens, and so fulfil the law of Christ.

(Galatians 6:10) **As we have therefore opportunity, let us do good unto all men, especially unto them who are of the household of faith.**

(Galatians 6:14) But God forbid that I should glory, save in the cross of our Lord Jesus Christ, by whom the world is crucified unto me, and I unto the world.

(Ephesians 3:13) Wherefore I desire that ye faint not at my tribulations for you, which is your glory.

(Ephesians 3:17-19) **That Christ may dwell in your hearts by faith; that ye, being rooted and grounded in love,**
May be able to comprehend with all saints what is the breadth, and length, and depth, and height;
And to know the love of Christ, which passeth knowledge, that ye might be filled with all the fulness of God.

(Ephesians 4:2) **With all lowliness and meekness, with longsuffering, forbearing one another in love;**

(Ephesians 4:15) But **speaking the truth in love, may grow up into him in all things,** which is the head, even Christ:

(Ephesians 4:32) **And be ye kind one to another, tenderhearted, forgiving one another, even as God for Christ's sake hath forgiven you.**

(Ephesians 5:2) And **walk in love, as Christ also hath loved us,** and hath given himself for us an offering and a sacrifice to God for a sweetsmelling savour.

(Ephesians 6:22) Whom I have sent unto you for the same

purpose, that ye might know our affairs, and that he might comfort your hearts.

(Ephesians 6:24) Grace be with all them that love our Lord Jesus Christ in sincerity. Amen.

(Philippians 1:3-5) I thank my God upon every remembrance of you,
Always in every prayer of mine for you all making request with joy,
For your fellowship in the gospel from the first day until now;

(Philippians 1:7) Even as it is meet for me to think this of you all, because I have you in my heart; inasmuch as both in my bonds, and in the defence and confirmation of the gospel, ye all are partakers of my grace.

(Philippians 1:8) For God is my record, how greatly I long after you all in the bowels of Jesus Christ.

(Philippians 1:9) And this I pray, that your love may abound yet more and more in knowledge and in all judgment;

(Philippians 1:20-21) According to my earnest expectation and my hope, that in nothing I shall be ashamed, but that with all boldness, as always, so now also **Christ shall be magnified in my body, whether it be by life, or by death.**
For to me to live is Christ, and to die is gain.

(Philippians 1:23-26) For I am in a strait betwixt two, having a desire to depart, and to be with Christ; which is far better:
Nevertheless to abide in the flesh is more needful for you.
And having this confidence, I know that I shall abide and continue with you all for your furtherance and joy of faith;
That your rejoicing may be more abundant in Jesus Christ for me by my coming to you again.

(Philippians 2:2) Fulfil ye my joy, that ye be likeminded, having the same love, being of one accord, of one mind.

(Philippians 2:19) But I trust in the Lord Jesus to send Timotheus shortly unto you, that I also may be of good comfort, when I know your state.

(Philippians 3:7-8) **But what things were gain to me, those I counted loss for Christ.**

Yea doubtless, and I count all things but loss for the excellency of the knowledge of Christ Jesus my Lord: for whom I have suffered the loss of all things, and do count them but dung, that I may win Christ,

(Philippians 3:18) **(For many walk, of whom I have told you often, and now tell you even weeping, that they are the enemies of the cross of Christ:**

(Philippians 4:1) Therefore, my brethren, dearly beloved and longed for, my joy and crown, so stand fast in the Lord, my dearly beloved.

(Colossians 1:3) **We give thanks to God and the Father of our Lord Jesus Christ, praying always for you,**

(Colossians 1:4) Since we heard of your faith in Christ Jesus, and of the love which ye have to all the saints,

(Colossians 1:8) Who also declared unto us your love in the Spirit.

(Colossians 1:24) Who now rejoice in my sufferings for you, and fill up that which is behind of the afflictions of Christ in my flesh for his body's sake, which is the church:

(Colossians 1:28-29) **Whom we preach, warning every man, and teaching every man in all wisdom; that we may present every man perfect in Christ Jesus:**

Whereunto I also labour, striving according to his working, which worketh in me mightily.

(Colossians 2:1-2) For I would that ye knew what great conflict I have for you, and for them at Laodicea, and for as many as have not seen my face in the flesh;

That their hearts might be comforted, being knit together in love, and unto all riches of the full assurance of understanding, to the acknowledgment of the mystery of God, and of the Father, and of Christ;

(Colossians 2:5) For though I be absent in the flesh, yet am I with you in the spirit, joying and beholding your order, and the stedfastness of your faith in Christ.

(Colossians 3:12-14) Put on therefore, as the elect of God, holy and beloved, bowels of mercies, kindness, humbleness of mind, meekness, longsuffering;
Forbearing one another, and forgiving one another, if any man have a quarrel against any: even as Christ forgave you, so also do ye.
And above all these things put on charity, which is the bond of perfectness.

(Colossians 4:7) All my state shall Tychicus declare unto you, who is a beloved brother, and a faithful minister and fellowservant in the Lord:

(1 Thessalonians 1:3-4) Remembering without ceasing your work of faith, and labour of love, and patience of hope in our Lord Jesus Christ, in the sight of God and our Father;
Knowing, brethren beloved, your election of God.

(1 Thessalonians 2:7-8) But we were gentle among you, even as a nurse cherisheth her children:
So being affectionately desirous of you, **we were willing to have imparted unto you, not the gospel of God only, but also our own souls, because ye were dear unto us.**

(1 Thessalonians 2:11-12) As ye know how we exhorted and comforted and charged every one of you, as a father doth his children,
That ye would walk worthy of God, who hath called you unto his kingdom and glory.

(1 Thessalonians 2:17-20) But we, brethren, being taken from you for a short time in presence, not in heart, endeavoured the more abundantly to see your face with great desire.
Wherefore we would have come unto you, even I Paul, once and again; but Satan hindered us.
For what is our hope, or joy, or crown of rejoicing? Are not even ye in the presence of our Lord Jesus Christ at his coming?
For ye are our glory and joy.

(1 Thessalonians 3:5) For this cause, when I could no longer forbear, I sent to know your faith, lest by some means the tempter have tempted you, and our labour be in vain.

(1 Thessalonians 3:7-10) Therefore, brethren, we were comforted over you in all our affliction and distress by your faith:
For now we live, if ye stand fast in the Lord.
For what thanks can we render to God again for you, for all the joy wherewith we joy for your sakes before our God;
Night and day praying exceedingly that we might see your face, and might perfect that which is lacking in your faith?

(1 Thessalonians 3:12) And the Lord make you to increase and abound in love one toward another, and toward all men, even as we do toward you:

(1 Thessalonians 4:9) But as touching brotherly love ye need not that I write unto you: for ye yourselves are taught of God to love one another.

(1 Thessalonians 5:8) But let us, who are of the day, be sober, putting on the breastplate of faith and love; and for an helmet, the hope of salvation.

(1 Thessalonians 5:11) Wherefore comfort yourselves together, and edify one another, even as also ye do.

(1 Thessalonians 5:14) Now we exhort you, brethren, warn them that are unruly, comfort the feebleminded, support the weak, be patient toward all men.

(2 Thessalonians 1:4) So that we ourselves glory in you in the churches of God for your patience and faith in all your persecutions and tribulations that ye endure:

(2 Thessalonians 3:5) And the Lord direct your hearts into the love of God, and into the patient waiting for Christ.

(1 Timothy 1:5) Now the end of the commandment is charity out of a pure heart, and of a good conscience, and of faith unfeigned:

(1 Timothy 1:14) And the grace of our Lord was exceeding abundant with faith and love which is in Christ Jesus.

(1 Timothy 2:15) Notwithstanding she shall be saved in childbearing, if they continue in faith and charity and holiness with sobriety.

(1 Timothy 4:12) Let no man despise thy youth; but be thou an example of the believers, in word, in conversation, in charity, in spirit, in faith, in purity.

(1 Timothy 5:9-10) Let not a widow be taken into the number under threescore years old, having been the wife of one man,
Well reported of for good works; if she have brought up children, if she have lodged strangers, if she have washed the saints' feet, if she have relieved the afflicted, if she have diligently followed every good work.

(1 Timothy 6:2) And they that have believing masters, let them not despise them, because they are brethren; but rather do them service, because they are faithful and beloved, partakers of the benefit. These things teach and exhort.

(1 Timothy 6:10-11) For the love of money is the root of all evil: which while some coveted after, they have erred from the faith, and pierced themselves through with many sorrows.
But thou, O man of God, flee these things; and follow after righteousness, godliness, faith, love, patience, meekness.

(2 Timothy 1:3) I thank God, whom I serve from my forefathers with pure conscience, that without ceasing I have remembrance of thee in my prayers night and day;

(2 Timothy 1:4) Greatly desiring to see thee, being mindful of thy tears, that I may be filled with joy;

(2 Timothy 1:7) For God hath not given us the spirit of fear; but of power, and of love, and of a sound mind.

(2 Timothy 1:13) Hold fast the form of sound words, which thou hast heard of me, in faith and love which is in Christ Jesus.

(2 Timothy 2:10) Therefore I endure all things for the elect's sakes, that they may also obtain the salvation which is in Christ Jesus with eternal glory.

(2 Timothy 2:22) Flee also youthful lusts: but follow righteousness, faith, charity, peace, with them that call on the Lord out of a pure heart.

(2 Timothy 3:8) Now as Jannes and Jambres withstood Moses, · so do these also resist the truth: men of corrupt minds, reprobate concerning the faith.

(2 Timothy 4:8) Henceforth there is laid up for me a crown of righteousness, which the Lord, the righteous judge, shall give me at that day: and not to me only, but unto all them also that love his appearing.

(Titus 3:15) All that are with me salute thee. Greet them that love us in the faith. Grace be with you all. Amen.

(Philemon 1:5) Hearing of thy love and faith, which thou hast toward the Lord Jesus, and toward all saints;

(Philemon 1:8) Wherefore, though I might be much bold in Christ to enjoin thee that which is convenient,

(Philemon 1:9) Yet for love's sake I rather beseech thee, being such an one as Paul the aged, and now also a prisoner of Jesus Christ.

(Philemon 1:12) Whom I have sent again: thou therefore receive him, that is, mine own bowels:

(Philemon 1:16-21) Not now as a servant, but above a servant, a brother beloved, specially to me, but how much more unto thee, both in the flesh, and in the Lord?
If thou count me therefore a partner, receive him as myself.
If he hath wronged thee, or oweth thee ought, put that on mine account;
I Paul have written it with mine own hand, I will repay it: albeit I do not say to thee how thou owest unto me even thine own self besides.
Yea, brother, let me have joy of thee in the Lord: refresh my bowels in the Lord.
Having confidence in thy obedience I wrote unto thee, knowing that thou wilt also do more than I say.

(Hebrews 5:2) Who can have compassion on the ignorant, and on them that are out of the way; for that he himself also is compassed with infirmity.

(Hebrews 6:9-10) But, beloved, we are persuaded better things of you, and things that accompany salvation, though we thus speak.
For God is not unrighteous to forget your work and labour of love, which ye have showed toward his name, in that ye have ministered to the saints, and do minister.

(Hebrews 10:24) And let us consider one another to provoke unto love and to good works:

(Hebrews 13:1) Let brotherly love continue.

(Hebrews 13:2) Be not forgetful to entertain strangers: for thereby some have entertained angels unawares.

(Hebrews 13:3) Remember them that are in bonds, as bound with them; and them which suffer adversity, as being yourselves also in the body.

(Hebrews 13:22) And I beseech you, brethren, suffer the word of exhortation: for I have written a letter unto you in few words.

(James 1:12) Blessed is the man that endureth temptation: for when he is tried, he shall receive the crown of life, which the Lord hath promised to them that love him.

(James 1:27) Pure religion and undefiled before God and the Father is this, **To visit the fatherless and widows in their affliction,** and to keep himself unspotted from the world.

(James 2:5) Hearken, my beloved brethren, Hath not God chosen the poor of this world rich in faith, and heirs of the kingdom which he hath promised to them that love him?

(James 2:8) If ye fulfil the royal law according to the scripture, Thou shalt love thy neighbour as thyself, ye do well:

(1 Peter 1:8) Whom having not seen, ye love; in whom, though now ye see him not, yet believing, ye rejoice with joy unspeakable and full of glory:

(1 Peter 1:22) Seeing ye have purified your souls in obeying the truth through the Spirit unto unfeigned love of the brethren, see that ye love one another with a pure heart fervently:

(1 Peter 2:7) Unto you therefore which believe he is precious: but unto them which be disobedient, the stone which the builders disallowed, the same is made the head of the corner,

(1 Peter 2:17) Honour all men. Love the brotherhood. Fear God. Honour the king.

(1 Peter 3:8-9) Finally, be ye all of one mind, having compassion one of another, love as brethren, be pitiful, be courteous:
Not rendering evil for evil, or railing for railing: but contrariwise blessing; knowing that ye are thereunto called, that ye should inherit a blessing.

(1 Peter 4:8) And above all things have fervent charity among yourselves: for charity shall cover the multitude of sins.

(2 Peter 1:7) And to godliness brotherly kindness; and to brotherly kindness charity.

(1 John 2:5) But whoso keepeth his word, in him verily is the love of God perfected: hereby know we that we are in him.

(1 John 2:9-11) He that saith he is in the light, and hateth his brother, is in darkness even until now.
He that loveth his brother abideth in the light, and there is none occasion of stumbling in him.
But he that hateth his brother is in darkness, and walketh in darkness, and knoweth not whither he goeth, because that darkness hath blinded his eyes.

(1 John 2:15) Love not the world, neither the things that are in the world. If any man love the world, the love of the Father is not in him.

(1 John 3:11) For this is the message that ye heard from the beginning, that we should love one another.

(1 John 3:14) We know that we have passed from death unto life, because we love the brethren. He that loveth not his brother abideth in death.

(1 John 3:16-19) Hereby perccive we the love of God, because he laid down his life for us: and we ought to lay down our lives for the brethren.

But whoso hath this world's good, and seeth his brother have need, and shutteth up his bowels of compassion from him, how dwelleth the love of God in him?

My little children, let us not love in word, neither in tongue; but in deed and in truth.

And hereby we know that we are of the truth, and shall assure our hearts before him.

(1 John 3:23) And this is his commandment, That we should believe on the name of his Son Jesus Christ, and love one another, as he gave us commandment.

(1 John 4:7) Beloved, let us love one another: for love is of God; and every one that loveth is born of God, and knoweth God.

(1 John 4:11-12) Beloved, if God so loved us, we ought also to love one another.

No man hath seen God at any time. If we love one another, God dwelleth in us, and his love is perfected in us.

(1 John 4:16-21) And we have known and believed the love that God hath to us. God is love; and he that dwelleth in love dwelleth in God, and God in him.

Herein is our love made perfect, that we may have boldness in the day of judgment: because as he is, so are we in this world.

There is no fear in love; but perfect love casteth out fear: because fear hath torment. He that feareth is not made perfect in love.

We love him, because he first loved us.

If a man say, I love God, and hateth his brother, he is a liar: for he that loveth not his brother whom he hath seen, how can he love God whom he hath not seen?

And this commandment have we from him, That he who loveth God love his brother also.

(1 John 5:1-3) Whosoever believeth that Jesus is the Christ is born of God: and every one that loveth him that begat loveth him also that is begotten of him.

By this we know that we love the children of God, when we love God, and keep his commandments.

For this is the love of God, that we keep his commandments: and his commandments are not grievous.

(2 John 1:5-6) And now I beseech thee, lady, not as though I wrote a new commandment unto thee, but that which we had from the beginning, that we love one another.

And this is love, that we walk after his commandments. This is the commandment, That, as ye have heard from the beginning, ye should walk in it.

(Jude 1:21) Keep yourselves in the love of God, looking for the mercy of our Lord Jesus Christ unto eternal life.

(Revelation 2:4) Nevertheless I have somewhat against thee, because thou hast left thy first love.

INDEX

A

A Christmas Carol 43
Abram 86
acceptance 25
Addison, Joseph 78
affection 63
Africa 13, 41
agapao 61, 62, 63, 65
agape 54, 55, 61, 62, 63, 66, 72, 75, 78, 81, 83, 86
Ai, Yang-Chao 87
anger 23
Augustine, St. 73, 89
Ayr 20

B

bad temper 22
Baker, Sir Henry William 67
Barrie, James Matthew 39
belief 25
bickering 83
Blake, William 16, 21
Boileau, Nicolas 19
Booth, William 89
Brainerd, David 89
Brooks, Phillips 85
Browning, Elizabeth Barrett 30, 42, 84
Browning, Robert 18
Bunyan, John 89